The Humpty
Dumpty Syndrome

The Humpty Dumpty Syndrome

Putting Yourself Together Again

Patricia H. Rushford

Fleming H. Revell
A Division of Baker Book House
Grand Rapids, Michigan 49516

Published by Fleming H. Revell
a division of Baker Book House Company
P.O. Box 6287, Grand Rapids, MI 49516-6287

Printed in the United States of America

Library of Congress Cataloging-in-Publication Data

Rushford, Patricia H.
  The Humpty Dumpty syndrome : putting yourself together again / Patricia H. Rushford.
      p.   cm.
  ISBN 0-8007-5511-1
  1. Mental health—Religious aspects—Christianity. 2. Spiritual life—Christianity. 3. Forgiveness of sins. 4. Sanctification.
  I. Title
  BT732.4.R87 1994
  248.8'6—dc20   93-34753

To Corisa and Christopher

who helped me regain childhood
and showed me how to live whole (holy)

Contents

Acknowledgments   9
Introduction   11

Part One: The Great Fall

1. Cracked Eggs and Broken People   19
2. Living in a Broken World   27
3. At the Bottom of It All   43

Part Two: The Healing

4. Picking Up the Pieces   59
5. All the King's Men—and Women   73
6. Restoring the Soul   85

Part Three: Living a Whole (Holy) Life

7. Going Back to the Garden   99
8. A Prisoner of Fear   115
9. Breaking Out   123
10. Adjusting to the New You   131
11. Making New Commitments   141
12. As Little Children   150
13. Having a Sense of Purpose   160
14. Life in the Garden   168
15. The Centering   184

Notes   193

Acknowledgments

THANKS TO THE FOLLOWING:

The professors and staff of Western Evangelical Seminary for their excellence in graduate education: To Anthony Cassarella, Ph.D.; Francis Whiting, D.Min.; Donald Hohensee, Ph.D.; Pastor Stanley Johnson, Ph.D.; Al Stiefel, Ph.D.; and Professor Judy Schwanz for their spiritual, theological, and psychological insight and expertise.

To counselor Michelle Rowen and teacher Sandy Bjorkman for their professional input.

To Ron Rushford, Margo Power, Sharon Bumala, Sally Kauffman, and my Round Robin friends for their editorial assistance.

To pastors Gail Vonada and Richard Lindstrom, for their spiritual help and encouragement.

Introduction

I'VE BEEN WORKING ON THIS BOOK ALL MY LIFE, but actually began organizing and writing it three years ago. When people would ask me what I was writing, I wasn't certain how to answer. In a way, it's a how-to book that gives broken people help and encouragement, and offers ways to overcome adversity. *The Humpty Dumpty Syndrome* is also a self-help book in that it offers helpful hints for putting yourself back together again. On the other hand, it is a spiritual journey book. As you read, you'll find accounts of my own falls and brokenness, and discover the healing process through which God has taken me. More than these, however, it is a guide to wholeness.

The idea of finding wholeness may be a confusing concept to some of you. This, and other terms I use, such as *centering* or having a *sense of oneness* with God, may seem foreign. Some of you may have heard them in the "new age" context and feel uncomfortable with them.

Another misconstrued term is *meditation*. Because the art of meditation has been linked with mysticism and eastern religions, some Christians run from it. What foolish-

ness. Meditation and prayer were very much a part of the
early Christian life and were exemplified by Christ.

I don't believe that by using certain buzz words we are
dancing with the devil. Quite frankly, I feel the opposite is
true. We are bowing to Satan by allowing him to distort
our words, thoughts, and symbols.

Because of some of the analogies and words I have chosen to use in writing *The Humpty Dumpty Syndrome*, and
because of some of the reactions I get when sharing them,
I thought it might be wise to define a few of them here in
the introduction.

Wholeness or *whole.* You will notice I often use whole
and holy synonymously. That is because you cannot be
whole until or unless you are holy. The root word for whole
is *hale,* as in hale and hearty. If we are to be whole—that
is healthy in body, mind, and spirit—we must also be holy.
The opposite of wholeness is brokenness. The opposite of
holy is unholiness (a state of being broken or separated
from God).

Centering. Toward the end of the book I've included a
chapter on centering. This term too has been misconstrued
by some as belonging to the "new age." By using it, I am
not promoting some mystical philosophy. I use it simply
because, through pottery and the concept of centering clay
on the wheel, God revealed some important principles. The
main point of centering is this: Being centered or focused
on God and submitting ourselves to him is our only hope
for true wholeness.

A sense of oneness. I use oneness to explain the feeling
I get when I *know* God in the most intimate sense. It is
entering into a covenant with God in much the same way
a man and woman enter into a covenant of marriage—the
idea of being Christ's bride. We can only experience oneness when we turn from sin and turn toward God.

We open ourselves to God and the Holy Spirit enters us;
then we are no longer two, but one (Gen. 3:24). Paul alludes

to this sense of oneness when he says, "In Him [Christ] we live and move and have our being" (Acts 17:28 NKJV); and "It is no longer I who live, but Christ lives in me" (Gal. 2:20 NKJV).

Too, it is the idea of growing Christ-like—of taking on godly attributes and becoming holy. I also talk about oneness in the merging of God's spirit with ours. In the Gospel of John, Christ uses the analogy of the vine and branches. "I am the Vine and you are the branches. He who abides in Me, and I in him, bears much fruit."

We may strive for wholeness, centeredness, and oneness with God, but we cannot attain them through our own efforts. They come as we release our hold, cease our struggles, and give ourselves up to the perfect will of God. It sounds simple, but as many of you know, it is not. My hope is that *The Humpty Dumpty Syndrome: Putting Yourself Together Again* will help you as you journey into wholeness, and that along the way you'll find the peace, joy, and happiness that only being whole can bring.

Part One

The Great Fall

Humpty Dumpty sat on a wall.
Humpty Dumpty had a great fall.
All the king's horses and all the king's men
Couldn't put Humpty together again.

As I READ THIS FAMILIAR RHYME ALOUD, five-year-old Corisa gazed at a picture of the fallen egg, dressed in a bow tie and red vest, and shook her head. "Why did Humpty fall, Nanna?" she asked.

"What do you think?" I asked.

Corisa shrugged. "Prob'ly 'cause he was naughty."

"No." Her cousin Christopher, also five, scowled.

"He wasn't naughty; he falled."

"Hmmm," I said. "Maybe you're both right."

"Why couldn't they fix him?" Christopher asked. Chris had the notion that just about anything could be fixed and he was just the guy to do it.

"Good question," I said. "Why do you think?"

Corisa giggled. "'Cause he's an egg, silly." At that our philosophical discussion gave way to play and we all crumpled in on each other, laughing about naughty eggs who fall off walls. But I kept wondering about Humpty. Why did he fall? Why couldn't all the king's horses and all the king's men put him back together again?

"Humpty Dumpty" is more than a simple rhyme to entertain children. Scholars claim its age can be measured in thousands of years, and suggest that the rhyme may have been written to express negative political views toward a reigning monarch or dictator.[1]

I see another message in this rhyme. The egg, symbolic of life, is broken, reminding us of our human frailty and the spills we take when life goes wrong. Humpty, the roly-poly egg-like man from our Mother Goose days, also represents humankind's great fall into sin and banishment from Eden, the perfect environment God had created for us. Humpty can be seen as a metaphor of the brokenness that plagues us both as individuals and as a society.

Have you ever fallen off the wall? Have you ever felt like Humpty—broken, shattered, coming apart? Have you ever felt as though you were exposed and bleeding, that even though your world was full of people who wanted to help and theories that promised to make you well, the most you received was a temporary fix?

This is a book about the falls and subsequent brokenness we experience in life and how they affect us emotionally and spiritually. As we look for ways to put our fractured selves back together again, we'll seek answers to some age-old questions:

What does it mean to be broken?
How does it feel?
How badly are we hurt?
How did we fall?

Why did it happen?

Can we ever be completely healed?

You'll discover ways of putting yourself together again—
that can lead to inner peace, happiness, and wholeness.
*The Humpty Dumpty Syndrome: Putting Yourself Together
Again* is not a prescription for happy-ever-after endings,
but a guide that offers realistic hope and stability in a
world that seems to be falling down around us.

Humpty's life was a mess. Unfortunately, far too many
people's lives are like that of the broken egg. Humpty's
story ended in tragedy, but we still have time to change
the end of our rhymes.

We can reverse the Humpty Dumpty Syndrome. If we
serve the right King, and if we have access to the right
methods, we *can* put ourselves and others back together
again. We can move beyond brokenness and frailty and
become fully restored—emotionally, spiritually, and perhaps even physically.[2]

1

Cracked Eggs
and Broken People

"WHY DOES LIFE HAVE TO BE SO HARD?" asked Kathy, my long-time friend. "Here I am, thirty-five years old. I finally thought I'd found the right guy. I felt really alive and happy for the first time in ten years. Jeff treated me like I was special. Then all of a sudden he's gone. Said he just didn't want to be married any more."

Kathy stroked the flop-eared bunny imprinted on her cup. Unable or unwilling to meet my eyes, she stared at the pine-paneled wall behind me. "I keep going over and over it. Were the kids too much for him? I know they can be a handful, but they're just normal, healthy kids. It has to be me. Was it something I said? Did I expect too much from him? You're a counselor, tell me what's wrong with me." Kathy put her cup on the table, leaned forward, and cradled her head in her hands.

Wanting to lessen her pain, I placed my hand on her arm and said, "You're being pretty hard on yourself."

She sniffed, and I stuffed a Kleenex into her hand. Without raising her head she wiped at her face. "I'm sorry you're hurting," I said. "I wish there was something I could do."

Kathy's lips curled in a half smile. "You're listening . . . that helps." She straightened and took a sip of her lukewarm coffee. Then, as if on automatic pilot, she rose, walked to the pot on the counter, and poured a fresh cup. "You want some more tea water?"

I nodded, sensing she needed to distance herself from her pain—needed time to pull her thoughts together.

A few minutes later, Kathy lowered herself into her chair. "You know what I can't understand? Why these things keep happening. I mean, my life reads like a soap opera. Things couldn't be worse if I had planned it. My counselor says maybe I'm afraid of success."

"Are you?"

"I don't think I'm afraid of succeeding. I'm not even sure what success is any more. It's more like I'm trying to fill something inside me . . . or fix a part of me that's not right. You know, like an empty space inside that needs . . . someone . . . something . . . maybe. Oh, I don't know. Sometimes I feel useless, like a broken toy that nobody wants."

We went on talking, Kathy and I, about needing to be affirmed and respected, about hurt, emptiness, loneliness, and being broken. Kathy is one of millions of broken people scattered across our world. Just as his great fall shattered Humpty, we too frequently find ourselves, our friends, and our families falling apart and badly in need of repair. But who will put us together again? Who will stop the despair that stalks us from generation to generation? Is there any hope?

Yes. Both help and hope are available for all of us, no matter how critical our condition. Healing is possible but not easily attained. Reversing the Humpty Dumpty Syndrome involves a process that requires us to endure discomfort, make choices, and change the way we live.

Examining Our Wounds

The first step in the healing process is to examine our wounds. How hard and how far have we fallen? What is the extent of our injuries? Wound examination, though not a pleasant procedure, is vital to healing and wholeness as is evidenced in the story of twelve-year-old Joshua.

One afternoon Joshua had delivered his last newspaper. In his eagerness to get home, he spun his ten-speed bike around in the roadside gravel and collided with a pickup truck. The impact forced Joshua ten feet into the air. He bounced twice on the gravel before landing in the ditch. In the emergency room, the medical team gave Joshua a thorough examination. Joshua's injuries consisted of a broken arm along with multiple cuts, scrapes, and bruises.

One wound at a time, the doctor probed the torn flesh to remove imbedded dirt and gravel. He thoroughly cleansed the wounds with an iodine solution to kill bacteria and prevent infection, then finished his task with sutures and dressings. Joshua survived, and his wounds healed with little scarring.

When treating emotional and spiritual wounds, the principle is the same. If the doctor had not properly handled Joshua's injuries, they could have become infected. In an improperly treated wound, bacteria grows, the wound festers, and infection spreads into the bloodstream and throughout the body. Without intervention, these toxins can cause serious illness and even death.

Similarly, emotional and spiritual toxins such as guilt, shame, anger, self-doubt, depression, pride, and fear can poison the mind and kill the spirit. So even though the task may be unpleasant, discovering the source of our brokenness is a vital first step to healing.

Reenacting the Fall

To begin our wound assessment, we'll need to spend some time probing into the spiritual and emotional part of ourselves to determine what's wrong and how badly we've been broken. First, however, let's define what being broken really means.

One way to do that is to reenact Humpty's fall and note the results. At a church retreat I led recently, I divided the participants into small groups and gave them the following materials: one raw egg, soft flexible tissue paper, craft glue, and scissors. I then asked one person in each group to hold the egg a couple of feet from the ground, a countertop, or a dish and drop it. "Now that Humpty has fallen," I said, "let's examine the victim and discuss the results of the fall."

Here are some of their comments:

"Mine hardly broke at all," John said with a grin. "Just a scrunched-up end and a little egg white seeping through the cracks. I guess he's a tough one."

"Oh." Anne wrinkled her nose in disgust. "Mine is splattered all over the table."

"Looks like a hopeless case to me," Jeremy said as he stroked his chin and hunkered down beside his egg to assess the damage. "His yolk is broken and running into a crack."

"Yuk." Jeannette grimaced. "His shell is shattered in a million pieces. No wonder the king's horses and men gave up on him. We'll never be able to get this egg together. Let's just get some towels and throw this mess down the garbage disposal."

I told her that wasn't an option in our experiment and that after examining their eggs, they were to make like the king's horses and men and attempt to put their Humpties back together again.

I'll reveal the results of the egg-restoration project later. Now, however, it's time to examine our broken selves and think about what brokenness means to us.

Brokenness Defined

Most of us can point to at least one crisis or tragedy in our lives that has left us broken. Losses, abuse, divorce, abortion, rape, illness, addictions, and rejection are just a sampling of the causes people cite for their brokenness. For many, the brokenness is something that happened to them—the result of hurt caused by others. Martin, for example, says he fell apart when he learned his daughter had become a lesbian.

Others feel crushed by something they did to someone else. Helen, a recent convert to Christianity says, "I spent the last twenty years of my life as an alcoholic. I know God has forgiven me, but not a day goes by that I don't worry about how my addiction has affected my three children."

Rose, an elderly widow, suffers from Alzheimer's disease. For Rose and many other older adults and their families, aging brings about losses such as decline of health, positions, roles, freedom, homes, and jobs, as well as the deaths of friends and family members.

Being broken means different things to different people. While some of us have greater resiliency than others, everyone is affected. "What does it mean to be broken?" When I ask people that question, I receive myriad answers, all of which reflect the varying degrees of pain in their lives.

It's Losing Everything. Tim lost his job when his plant closed. After fifteen years of stability, he and his wife, Ann, suddenly found themselves facing economic disaster. They lost their house and nearly everything they owned. Perhaps even more significant, Tim's loss and inability to find work tore apart his sense of purpose and self-worth.

It's Like a Broken Heart. "It's like having a broken heart," said Jenny, a recent college graduate. "My whole world fell apart when Jason and I broke up. We'd planned to be married. I loved him so much. I feel discarded and so . . . empty."

Lisa, a twenty-eight-year-old kindergarten teacher said, "I was totally shattered when I lost my baby to SIDS (Sudden Infant Death Syndrome). I'm not sure I'll ever get over it."

It's Being a Victim. Mark, a pastor, said that he felt his brokenness was caused by an abusive father: "If he didn't have anything better to do, he'd beat me up. I think he enjoyed it . . . getting drunk and terrorizing Mom and me. Part of me is okay, but there's a little kid in me that never had a chance."

"For me," Carla, a homemaker and mother of five admitted, "it's watching my teenage sons practically destroy themselves. Michael marched into his teens like a military commando, shooting his mouth off at anyone who happened to be in his line of fire. He's gotten into alcohol and drugs. Sean is following in his older brother's footsteps. Sometimes I blame their father—and God—but most of all I blame myself. I've been hurt before, but never like this. I feel as though the life is being crushed out of me."

Broken in Childhood

Pain has no boundaries and no respect for age. Many people I talked with or read about while doing research for this book said they had been broken in childhood.

According to the Children's Defense Fund, "A child is abused or neglected every 47 seconds in the US."[1] Great strides have been made toward reform and stricter laws governing child safety and the rights of children. Yet even today, millions of children around the world are unloved, neglected, abandoned, abused, and even murdered. And countless more are damaged in ways which we may not even be aware. Sometimes they are even broken by those who are trying to stop the brokenness.

One story that comes to mind is that of Denise, a single parent whose two-year-old daughter was taken away from her when she was falsely accused of child abuse. A year later, Denise won her case, but her healthy baby had been broken by the loss of her loving mommy. Her once outgoing, talkative toddler returned a ". . . clingy little girl who fears strangers, cries out in her sleep, and wants to be cuddled constantly."

"Mommy," the child cries, "my heart has been so empty of you because you weren't there. Please hold me. Fill my heart back up."[2]

Some babies are broken before birth. Andy is a victim of fetal alcohol syndrome because his smother drank alcohol during her pregnancy. Casey's mom spaced out on crack. Even if the womb in which we develop is comforting and nurturing, we fall into the world, bloody and bruised. We enter an often cold and hostile environment where disease, child abuse, abortions, beatings, rape, and murder are as common as the six-o-clock news.

The number of people in our country with relationship problems, personality disorders, addictions and dependency issues, history of abuse, chronic depression, suicidal tendencies and other afflictions is growing at an alarming rate. Tragically, these fractured and broken people pass their own brand of brokenness on to their children, and so it goes from generation to generation as we learn what we live.

All of us, to greater and lesser degrees, come from dysfunctional family systems. Mental health professionals sag under the weight of dealing with too many people with too many wounds and too little time.

Uncovering Your Brokenness

In this chapter we've looked into the lives of a number of people who know how it feels to be broken. Now it's time for some introspection on your part.

To aid you in the healing process, I suggest you keep a journal entitled "My Journey to Wholeness." As you read this book, pause periodically to reflect and write journal entries about your own brokenness and wounds that need healing. Note inspiring Bible verses, quotes, and insights gained as you read, and include methods you feel will facilitate your healing process.

Below I've listed three questions to help you examine your wounds. Write your answers and any other thoughts that come to mind in your journal.

1. What does being broken mean to you?
2. Can you recall a time or incident in your life that damaged you?
3. How does your brokenness keep you from the following:
   a. being satisfied with life?
   b. feeling good about yourself?
   c. maintaining healthy relationships?

In this chapter we've examined our wounds and discussed what it means to be broken. Perhaps you wonder, as do most of us, why there is so much pain. Why doesn't God do something? Why have so many fallen? Why do we, despite the help available, often find ourselves in pieces?

We'll attempt to find some answers to these questions and more as we move into chapter 2 and probe more deeply into our hurts to discover the source of our pain.

2

Living in a Broken World

SOME TIME AGO, MY HUSBAND AND I took our grandson Christopher, then five, with us on a trip that included a visit to Custer's Battlefield in Montana. White tombstones littered the countryside, telling of a tragic war between Native Americans and the U.S. Cavalry. We listened as one of the "ghost tenders" (a term local Indians used to describe the park rangers), told us how the Indians, in an effort to protect their land and families, destroyed Custer's entire troop.

As the ranger told about the battle and the lives lost, Christopher tugged at my hand and asked, "Why did it hafta happen, Nanna?"

Why indeed? I knelt beside him and retold the story in words I hoped he could understand. When I finished he looked at me again, his enormous brown eyes shadowed with concern. "But why did it happen?"

Why Did It Happen?

Why is there so much pain in the world? Why do we fight in wars that should never have begun? Why do people suffer?

During a retreat one spring, a conferee gifted me with a large blue button that read, "Humpty Dumpty was pushed!" Is that the answer? Are we all victims of a hostile environment that pushes us over the edge? Or is there something more? Let's probe the ruins of our fallen world and find out.

Obvious Cracks and Gaping Holes

The local evening news and other TV programs reveal all too clearly the shattered state of humanity. Our nation is in economic crisis. Political opponents verbally assassinate one another in an effort to prove their worth to the voting public.

The press hovers over us like hungry vultures, waiting for scandalous stories to break. Sordid details of rape and murder trials and executions consume the airwaves. Spectators choose sides and cheer the players on as if they were indulging a game.

Men and women attack one another in a struggle for recognition and power. Daily our television screens and newspapers relate the horrors of homelessness, poverty, nuclear threats, robbery, rape, child abuse, and drive-by shootings.

But perhaps even worse than the news is our reaction to it. Some of us watch with mild anger and concern, wishing we could do something. Some take it in, store it along with the millions of other tragic cases, and try to forget. Others, out of apathy, desensitization, or perhaps fear and a sense of hopelessness, switch to an old sitcom. A few— those who still believe in miracles, those whose passion has not been spent—dedicate their lives to picking up the pieces and trying to make things better.

At this point, you may want to make a few notations in your journal as you consider these questions.

1. As you look around you, what evidence do you see of a broken, decaying world?
2. Have you suffered as a result of a world gone bad?
3. Have you or has someone close to you been violated? In what way?

A World Gone Bad

We, who were created in God's image and chosen to represent God on Earth, suffer from feelings of inadequacy, worthlessness, depression, lack of control, rejection, and low self-esteem. Emptiness, loneliness, anger, pride, grief, guilt, greed, and hatred push us dangerously close to the edge of our emotional safety zones. We're split apart by the lack of intimacy and by sexual promiscuity, divorce, racism, and sexism. The rising incidences of child abuse, abandonment, and abortion shatter us. Debilitating and deadly diseases such as AIDS and cancer infect us. Thieves, rapists, and murderers crush us with their evil deeds. And we're left wondering if there is any hope at all.

Considering all the evil in the world, it's a wonder we're still alive. Amazingly, as we examine the wounds of the world, we find that woven into the dark tragedy of it all are golden fibers of faith, hope, and love that hold the fabric of humankind together. These and God and perhaps the will to live seem, at times, the only things that keep us from being completely destroyed.

We have mentioned only a few of the problems that debilitate our world. Certainly it is in critical condition. Are we broken because we live in a broken world? Are we innocent victims and casualties of a world gone bad? More likely, the world is broken because it is full of broken people.

This takes us back to Christopher's question at the beginning of this chapter: "Why?" If we are to learn why we are broken, we must look beyond ourselves and even beyond the world we live in.

Broken All the Way Down

Finding the source of our brokenness is like trying to discover which came first, the chicken or the egg. After delivering a philosophy lecture, William James was confronted by an elderly woman who claimed to have discovered the answer to the cause-and-effect dilemma.

> "We don't live on a ball rotating around the sun," she theorized. "We live on a crust of earth on the back of a giant turtle."
>
> James was silent for a moment, then answered, "If your theory is correct, madam, what does the turtle stand on?"
>
> "The first turtle stands on the back of a second, far larger turtle, of course," she said.
>
> "But what does this second turtle stand on?"
>
> "It's no use, Mr. James," she said with finality. "It's turtle all the way down."[1]

While I don't believe, as our would-be philosopher, that "it's *turtle* all the way down," I do think there is a basic underlying cause of the prevailing brokenness in our world. So perhaps in searching for answers to our brokenness, we need to begin with the premise that *we are broken all the way down.* The cosmic egg is cracked and we're fractured to the core.

To get to the bottom of it all, we need to probe even more deeply into the scattered remains of our Humpty Dumpty selves. Like detectives in a murder mystery, we'll want to investigate the fall, examine Humpty's remains, and dig into his past. We'll try to determine why he was on the wall and how he fell. Was he pushed? Did he jump? What precipitated the fall? What was life like for Humpty before the tragedy occurred?

We know from the story that Humpty fell. We also know that at one time Humpty sat on the wall. We can surmise that in the beginning he was intact, a complete and whole being. Here human beings find a common ground with Humpty, for we, too, were once whole and complete, lacking in nothing. Humankind, in the beginning, lived in a world where everything was good and right and perfect.

Created in God's Image

To answer some of our questions, let's go back to the beginning of human existence and consider the way we were before the fall. To do this, take out the "family album," better known as the Bible. As we open the book, the first pictures we see are of God as an expectant Father. With loving care, God created a perfect environment for his children. Out of nothing except the power of his Word, he created mountains and valleys, oceans and streams. He hung the heavens and ordered the earth to produce every kind of vegetation. He created birds, animals, and creatures to fill the seas. It was all good—well ordered and perfectly balanced.

The care God took to make a place for us reminds me of nurturing parents who painstakingly prepare a nursery for their new baby, wanting everything to be just right when the child arrives.

When God had created the perfect environment and all was in place, God said:

> Let us make [humans] in our image, after our likeness; and let them have dominion over the fish of the sea, and over the birds of the air, and over the cattle, and over all the

earth, and over every creeping thing. . . . So God created [humans] in his *own* image; in the image of God he created [humanity]; male and female he created them. And God blessed them.   Genesis 1:26–28, emphasis added

God saw everything that he had made, and behold, it was very good.   Genesis 1:31

Humankind is created in the image of God—the *Imago Dei*. The implications of that statement are phenomenal. For a graduate-school theology class I wrote a paper entitled "The *Imago Dei*: Discovering Human Identity." One of my first tasks was to define the phrase so I could gain a clearer understanding of what it means to be created in the image of God.

In *Webster's New World Dictionary of the American Language,* I discovered that "image" (*imago*) means a "likeness, imitation, copy . . . a representation of a person . . . the visual representation of something produced by reflection from a mirror . . . a counterpart. "Of God" (*Dei*) means "to gleam, shine; divine nature."

From these definitions we see that men and women were created to reflect the fullness of God's glory. Theologian Charles Carter states, ". . . humanity bears God's image in the everlastingness of his Being."[2]

In the beginning Adam and Eve were holy, eternal beings. They were whole, fully competent, functional, confident in body, soul, and spirit. They were fully relational to self, to one another, and to God.

In this state of wholeness they were free to love and to be themselves. They didn't have to ask the question "Who am I?" because they already knew. They clearly saw themselves reflecting God's image as if looking in a spotless mirror. God, man, and woman functioned as a complete and flawless family unit, living in perfect harmony with themselves and with one another.

Can you imagine what it must have been like—to live in so intimate a relationship with God? There were no cracks—no anger, guilt, or greed. Adam and Eve had no identity problems, no poor self-esteem, no sense of inadequacy. They knew the truth—that God loved and valued them above all other creatures—and out of that love they were able to fully love one another. Humanity, in its perfect state of wholeness and love reflected God's glory.

At this point I'd like you to take out your journal again and imagine what life might have been like in the Garden. Then enter your impressions.

The Fall

The first part of Genesis reads like a fairy tale. God wanted everything to be perfect for his flawless children. He provided for their needs and established boundaries to keep them safe and secure. Then something tragic happened and our ancestors, like Humpty Dumpty, fell from their holy place.

Why Did They Do It?

My granddaughter Corisa brought home a picture she'd made in preschool. "Nanna," she asked, "why did they do it?"

"Do what, Honey?" I hunkered down in front of her and looked at her masterpiece. The scene was a familiar one. Adam and Eve, having been seduced by the serpent, were eating the forbidden fruit, which in Corisa's picture looked like an apple.

"Why did they be naughty?" she inquired again.

"I don't know," I said honestly. "Do you know why you do naughty things sometimes?"

"Nope," she said. "But I'm little and they're big."

I smiled and hugged her. Old feelings of regret and anger washed over me as I pictured Adam and Eve doing the one thing God had asked them not to do. I tried to put myself in their place. Would I have succumbed to temptation and disobeyed God? If my own imperfections have any bearing on my answer, I'd have to say, "Probably."

Like Corisa, I wondered, "Why?"

As we read the creation story we discover all too soon that evil infiltrated Eden and turned contentment into chaos. What makes the story even more tragic is that Adam and Eve had a choice. In the fall, the most beautiful of creatures, formed by God's own hands, exercised their most powerful tool (free will) and made a decision that cost them their lives.

Why did they do it? They had it all—well almost. God had given them all they needed and established appropriate boundaries that would assure their safety and well-being. They lacked only one thing. The Bible tells us that God warned Adam and Eve, saying, "of the tree of the knowledge of good and evil you shall not eat, for in the day that you eat of it you shall die" (Gen. 2:17). Then another voice offered an alternative, and they listened to Satan rather than God.

Why did they do it? Perhaps Adam and Eve fell because they wanted more. Or maybe they fell because they wanted to be more like God. They desired more power, knowledge, independence, and wisdom. Whatever their reasons, they made a grave mistake and suffered the consequences. They walked too close to the edge. They went one step too far and fell into the darkness.

Separated from God

Did the wrong choice mean that they would be lost forever? What did God mean when he said they would die? Of course, eventually they did die, but not right away. The Bible shows that Adam and Eve went on to live long and productive lives. John Wesley made this observation:

"Accordingly, in that day he did die: He died to God,—the most dreadful of all deaths. He lost the life of God: He was separated from Him, in union with whom his spiritual life consisted. The body dies when it is separated from the soul; the soul, when it is separated from God."[3] Proof of that separation was evidenced in Adam's behavior. ". . . the love of God was extinguished in his soul, which was now alienated from God."[4]

The great fall from the Garden and separation from God caused a great deal of confusion and pain for the first humans. That confusion is still evident today.

We were never meant to live in an evil world. We were never meant to feel emotional pain or hardship. We were not created to hurt others. We were designed to be happy, healthy, and at peace with God, with ourselves, and with others. God designed us to live in a holy environment in which we could commune daily with him. Holiness was a part of our being. Because we were created this way, God was, is, and always will be as vital to our souls as oxygen is to our bodies. Without God we are lost, our image of God and of ourselves is distorted, and as such, we are continually trying to adjust to a world gone bad.

The Shattered Image

The choices our ancestors made affect us. In our broken state we look in the mirror and see our distorted selves, vaguely remembering what we used to look like. The longer we are broken the less visible our godly image becomes to us. But somewhere in the deepest part of our souls we do remember.

The Soul Remembers

The image of God in us, the perfect life we were meant to have for eternity, exists only as a distant memory. Our

souls grieve for what once was and seek desperately to pull
us back to the perfection we once had. Since we were not
created to be broken we cannot tolerate our condition.
Thus, we persistently seek to regain wholeness and cannot be truly satisfied until we achieve it.

Our spirits are drawn to visions of wholeness. Sometimes we even imagine ourselves being complete. Other
times we may look around at humanity and decide that,
since we all have faults, brokenness must be normal. But
it isn't. And if we're cunning enough we can even pretend
we never fell at all. But we did. And like the eggs we
dropped earlier, we are a mess.

Counting the Cost

The first humans went from being normal to being
abnormal—from being natural and whole to being unnat-
ural and broken. To fully understand what falling has done
to our personalities, relational abilities, and self-identi-
ties, we must closely consider our losses. William Kirwan,
in *Biblical Concepts for Christian Counseling,* gives an
excellent illustration of what humanity lost when they
sided against God and allied themselves with Satan.

> When Adam and Eve fell, they lost their harmonious rela-
> tionship with God, with the rest of creation, with one
> another, and even with their real selves. . . . When Adam
> told God that he hid because he was afraid, he was saying
> in essence, "I have lost God, so I no longer belong. I am
> afraid and insecure." He was also saying, "I have lost per-
> fection, so I no longer feel a sense of self-esteem. Instead I
> feel guilty and ashamed." God asked Adam, "Who told you
> that you were naked?" Of course, no one had. God was
> accentuating the fact that the shame Adam felt was self-
> caused. Adam brought it on himself, and he was feeling its
> consequences. Finally, Adam was saying, "I have lost con-
> trol, so I am weak and feel depressed." Before the fall, Adam
> was . . . strong enough to deal satisfactorily with any situ-

ation that might come his way . . . [meaning he was strong enough to resist *all* temptation, even the desire to be equal to God]. Now he no longer had that strength. He undoubtedly felt inferior and insignificant.[5]

The Lost Image

In the fall the children God so lovingly created were separated from their Father. The human soul lost intimacy with the Holy Spirit, and as a result all humankind suffers from brokenness, emptiness, inadequacy, rejection, shame, and helplessness.

We carry our pain, hunger, shame, anger, and guilt into every part of our lives and pass our legacy from generation to generation. At birth we fall into the arms of imperfect parents in an imperfect world. From the beginning we see ourselves from a human perspective rather than from God's.

The Hidden Self

We are unique creatures, equipped with our own personalities. We are human beings created in God's image, and we are as whole and complete as we can get in our broken world. As we grow and develop we are often guided by forces greater than ourselves. Some of those forces are positive, many are not. We are all too often forced to defend ourselves and to conform to a lifestyle that has no resemblance to the way God planned for us to live.

Entrapped we spend our lives fighting, defending, or giving in. Eventually, because we are shamed, bullied, and told not to be what we are, we lose our sense of trust, individuality, creativity, and unconditional love. Our godlike characteristics are covered with pride, bitterness, resentment, anger, and hate. We learn to be ashamed of ourselves because we are not what we could be. We become caught in a seemingly impossible dilemma, because, even though we are now unlovable and unacceptable, we must have love, we must be accepted, and we must maintain some semblance of identity.

When children are threatened, their strongest defense is to conform—to do whatever must be done to be accepted and loved. Or, as happens all too often, they rebel. And perhaps the rebels are the most honest. Perhaps these are the prophets God uses to show us how damaged we really are.

In either case, we stop being human beings and become humans doing whatever it takes to survive. We lock away the inner self and cover the image of God. Then, in order to be accepted, we conform and re-create ourselves in the image of broken people. Through manipulation or force, we struggle to gain control—to bring back the sense of self that seems to be steadily slipping away.

Our self-esteem is gained by comparing ourselves to others who appear to be even more broken than we. Out of a desperate desire to survive, we strut our so-called successes to the world. Like peacocks we arrange our brilliant blue feathers around us in the shape of a crown. We fashionably present ourselves and though we'd never say the words aloud, the message is clear. *Look what I've accomplished in spite of my brokenness. I've overcome great obstacles, be proud of me. I may not be perfect, but at least I'm not feeling sorry for myself.* We come to believe in the false self we present to others rather than the fractured hidden self created in the image of God.

We try to love this false self, and may even come to worship it, because there is a deep fear within us that warns, *If you destroy this self, there will be nothing left of you.* This destruction and love of the counterfeit self is narcissism.

Denying the True Self

Narcissism is not self-love. Rather, it is an egocentricity that denies and hides the true self. Adam and Eve, as God's image bearers, naturally had the ability to know, respect, and love themselves. That natural and spontaneous ability was distorted in the fall. Again the soul somehow recollects that we are supposed to love the self, so we try and fail. Unfortunately, we end up loving the wrong self.

According to Dr. Alexander Lowen in *Narcissism: Denial of the True Self,*

> Narcissists do not love themselves or anyone else. . . . Narcissism denotes a personality disturbance characterized by an exaggerated investment in one's self image at the expense of the self. . . . Narcissists are more concerned with how they appear than what they feel . . . they deny feelings that contradict the image they seek. Acting without feeling, they tend to be seductive and manipulative, striving for power and control. They are egotists, focused on their own interests but lacking the true values of the self—namely self-expression, self-possession, dignity, and integrity. Narcissists lack a sense of self derived from body feelings. Without a solid sense of self, they experience life as empty and meaningless. It is a desolate state.[6]

Narcissism is the love and nurturance of a self created in the human image rather than the God image. I used to struggle with the issue of self-esteem, trying desperately to find something about myself I could honestly love. No matter how many affirmations I repeated, no matter how often I said, "You're okay," it didn't ring true. Deep inside I knew something was wrong, I just didn't know what.

The struggle to understand the depth of our broken image is hampered by our own efforts to salvage what's left of us. But it is often crushed by a society so caught up in the worship of its false self it refuses to acknowledge the truth.

A False Culture

Divorce, abortion, child abuse, pornography, murder, rape, the quest for personal and spiritual power are signs

of devaluation and degradation of human life. Ours is a
society that believes in its image, praising and glorifying
youth, money, sex, and power. It has lost sight of and in
some cases even murdered and buried the self created in
God's own image.

Narcissism, then, is a driving passion to love the false
self and to give it a reason for existence. The false image
urgently tries to reproduce life before the fall, touting
wholeness, godlikeness, and love. As long as we look at one
another and the rest of the world, we may believe in our
image. But the moment we look at God, the instant we
allow his glory to illuminate our lives, we see how far from
perfect and acceptable we really are. No wonder Adam and
Eve hid from God. No wonder so many of us still do. To love
the wrong self is to deny God and to deny God is to destroy
the soul.

Soul Murder

John Bradshaw, in *Bradshaw On: The Family* says, "To
have one's feelings, body, desires and thoughts controlled
is to lose one's self. To lose one's self is to have one's soul
murdered."[7] When we control, manipulate, or try to erase
the true self in us and in others, when we deny the image
of God in us, we do indeed, murder the soul.

Eventually as we grow up, the "real" self is covered by
layers of pride, defenses, which form the "public" self. All
too often, the unique God-created image—the true self—
is so expertly hidden, we grow up never knowing who we
really are.

This public self goes through life equipped with false
beliefs, often making wrong choices, fighting for control,
but in actuality having none. We fall into compulsive,
addictive behavior patterns in an attempt to find our
identities and to cover up the shame and the loss of not
being real.

We See Ourselves Through Others' Eyes

Most personality theorists agree that identities are formed by how other people see us. If you see love and acceptance of yourself reflected in a parent's eyes, you see yourself as a lovable and acceptable person. If you see anger and criticism in their eyes, you see yourself as unworthy and unacceptable. How do you see yourself?

Write in your journal your impressions of this chapter.

1. How do you feel about having been created in God's image?
2. How do you see yourself at this point?
3. The self, the "I am," has been critically damaged in the fall. The identity we once had in God is at times clouded and distorted by evil. The more distant God is from us, the less sense of self reality we have. Close your eyes and imagine yourself as a character in a play. How would you describe yourself? What do you see? Write *I am . . .* and list ten attributes that most accurately describe you.

Sarah's "I am . . ." went like this:

I am a secretary, wife, mother, a homemaker. I am confused. Sometimes there's a shadow over me and I feel like I'm buried. I am dead, but I'm also alive. I'm not a nice person, not really. I do good things to convince myself and others there is something good about me. Sometimes I even believe it. I am . . . I don't think I really know who or what I am.

When I first began to write my I am . . . it was like Sarah's. I was in the middle of a depression and had difficulty seeing my true self. I am different now, not because I've taken classes on how to improve my image, but because my image has been restored and my soul made whole by God.

Evil polluted our perfect environment. It dropped like a black cloud between humanity and God, distorting our vision and leading us astray. The perfect peace and ability to relate that Adam and Eve had known so well was replaced with shame, guilt, and desperate attempts to preserve their fragile selves.

Knowing the Enemy

Perhaps at this point you're asking, "Is this really necessary? Why do I need to know all of this stuff about the fall and about sin? Can't we just get on with the healing part of this program?"

Unfortunately, no. Simply knowing that sin is behind our brokenness is not enough to facilitate a cure. Like Joshua, the boy who sustained multiple injuries in a truck-bike accident, we too must undergo a careful examination and deal with any contaminants imbedded in our wounds.

To beat the enemy, we must first know the enemy. If we are to be fully healed, we must first examine evil. Once we know what we are dealing with and understand the extent of the damage, we can begin the healing process.

Before we move into chapter 3, where we'll learn more about the dirt and debris in our lives, take a moment to consider the fall of humankind and how that fall still affects us today. Then write those reflections in your journal.

3

At the Bottom
of It All

CASEY, AGE SEVEN, SAT AT THE TOP OF THE STAIRS outside his room. He brushed away the last of his tears. "It isn't fair," he mumbled. He'd been sent to his room for something his three-year-old sister Sarah had done. Well, no matter— he'd get even.

The next morning, after his sister had gone downstairs to watch television and before his parents were awake, Casey redecorated the bathroom with toothpaste. Then he went back into his room and pretended to be asleep. Were it not for the sly grin on his face when Sarah got the blame, no one would ever have known who the real culprit was— except for Casey and, of course, God.

What a mischievous little guy. What would possess Casey to do something like that? Could it be sin? Is it possible children even as young as Casey and Sarah could be capable of committing sinful acts? Sadly, yes.

The Dirt in Our Souls

When Humpty fell, he was contaminated by dirt and debris and would never be the same again. Similarly, evil

43

contaminates every human and persistently tries to prevent us from living out our lives as God intended. As we saw in the last chapter, when Adam and Eve disobeyed God, sin penetrated their world.

Adam and Eve divorced God and entered into an adulterous relationship with Satan. The liaison between humanity and evil brought sin into the world. Evil is widespread and devastating, but God has given us the power to overcome it.

In Genesis 4:7 God says, "If you do well, will you not be accepted? And if you do not do well, sin lies at the door. And its desire is for you, but you should rule over it" (NKJV).

That's good news for us. Just as the doctor was able to wash out the dirt and gravel imbedded in Joshua's wounds, sin can be cleansed from our souls. We begin the cleansing by examining the nature of sin.

Throughout the ages prophets, preachers, philosophers, and ordinary people have struggled to understand the presence of evil in the world. Theologian Charles W. Carter says, "of all the problems confronting humanity, evil is the most universal, vexing and enigmatic [baffling]."[1] In our confusion we ask:

- Was evil present from the beginning of time?
- Did God create evil?
- When and why did sin come into our world?
- How do we define evil?
- How deeply are we affected by it?
- Can we overcome it?

Before we go on to explore these concerns, take a moment to reflect on the following questions and note your impressions in your journal.

1. Is there a dark side of your life (some dirt in your soul) you don't want anyone to see? Write about your inner darkness.

2. Without looking it up, and in your own words, define sin.
3. According to your definition, are you a sinner? How does that make you feel?
4. What kinds of sins have you committed?
5. Have you ever felt oppressed by evil or driven to do something you knew was wrong or harmful to yourself or others?

The Origin of Evil

In Eden, Satan seduced Eve and Adam. The creature lied to them, promising enlightenment and giving only darkness. Unfortunately, Satan continues to tempt us today. But where did this evil influence come from?

Theories on the origin of evil abound. Some say it is eternal; others regard it as a cosmic accident. Some say evil is the necessary antithesis of good. Others say it is the physical nature opposing the spiritual, while still others view evil as coming out of moral ignorance.[2]

Charles W. Carter writes, "The Bible represents evil at the outset as an immoral act of disobedience, rather than a cosmic accident."[3] Evil can have no power unless we yield to it. Humanity has the freedom to choose whether or not to respond to evil. Even though Satan battles for our souls, we are not pawns in an eternal game between the forces of good and evil or between God and Satan. Even though things happen over which we have no control, we are responsible for our choices and are held accountable for our decisions and actions.

The First to Fall

In the Genesis account, Satan appeared to Eve and Adam as a serpent, not as an internal feeling. This tells us that evil existed before humans were created. Merrill F. Unger, in his book *Demons in the World Today,* says:

> It was the intrusion of Satan's will against the divine will that introduced sin into a sinless universe and transformed "Lucifer" (Lightbearer) into "Satan" (Opposer). Satan's rebellion fixed the pattern of satanic and demonic attitude as opposition to God and exaltation of self.[4]

Some have suggested that evil developed out of Lucifer's opposition to God. Lucifer, the most beautiful and highly regarded of God's angels, became enamored with itself and enthralled with its own power and turned against God. References to fallen angels suggest that Lucifer did not go down alone. In 2 Peter 2:4 we read that "God did not spare the angels when they sinned, but cast them into hell and committed them to pits of nether gloom to be kept until the judgment" (RSV). Jude 6 tells of "angels that did not keep their own position, but left their proper dwelling."

We don't know for certain how it all happened, or why. What we can be certain of is that evil does exist. The Bible clearly indicates the presence of Satan, the Prince of Darkness, and of demons.

Demons and Darkness

Demons are nonhuman and do not have physical bodies. Being spirits, they cannot harm us unless we allow them to use or enter our bodies. Dr. Unger writes, "Invisible, extremely intelligent, strong, and totally depraved personalities can do a great deal of damage to the unregenerate [non-spiritual, defiant] person, leading him into evil (Eph. 2:2–3; Col. 1:13)."[5] If we allow them, demons can use us to hurt others and to oppose God.

Demons can attack, oppress, and in some cases even possess people. The apostle Paul reminds us that "we are not contending against flesh and blood, but against the principalities, against the powers, against the world rulers of this present darkness . . ." (Eph. 6:12).[6]

Wayne E. Caldwell says this in his discussion on demonology (the study of demons):

> Probably at no point in theology has there been a greater misuse or abuse of the imagination than in the speculation surrounding Satan—his origin, character, and existence. The human imagination seems always more fertile when dealing with evil than when dealing with good. Perhaps this is so because evil is less evil in imagination than reality, whereas good is always better in reality than in imagination.[7]

You have probably read stories or seen films depicting demons as scaly, dragonlike creatures that sit on people's shoulders and cause them to do terrible things. In *This Present Darkness,* author Frank Peretti gave us a glimpse into what the spiritual world might be like if demons could be seen. His book became a bestseller, possibly because the story, while fictitious, contains elements of truth regarding the reality of the power of evil and our human need to overcome it.

While we recognize that evil spirits exist, we should be careful not to overemphasize the power and presence of demons or take a "demon-on-every-doorknob" approach. We can be too quick to blame demons for our wrong choices.

Not long ago, I heard a man tell how he'd been delivered from the demon of lust. I've heard others talk about the demon of fear, the demon of alcoholism, the demon of depression and so on. Even overeating has been demonized. I'm reminded of a comedian who, every time he did something wrong, would say, "The devil made me do it."

While demonic forces may be intrusive, we need to remember our power over them: Without our consent, the devil can't *make us* do anything. Unfortunately, Satan has done an excellent job of convincing us otherwise.

Our imaginations can either expand or dilute our perception of evil, and that is a dangerous thing. In *The Screwtape Letters* C. S. Lewis states:

> There are two equal and opposite errors into which our race can fall about the devils. One is to disbelieve in their existence. The other is to believe, and to feel an excessive and unhealthy interest in them. They themselves are equally pleased by both errors and hail a materialist or a magician with the same delight.[8]

Evil is an ever-present danger and should never be taken lightly. It is manifested and made powerful by human weakness and lack of understanding. The rulers of darkness relentlessly pursue us and take advantage of our weakness and ignorance in trying to separate us from God.

According to Dr. William Kirwan, "Sin must always be viewed in the context of a broken relationship with God."[9] If this is true, we need to look at evil not as a dragonlike entity sitting on one's shoulder, but as a fast-growing, invasive cancer that can devastate our lives. Sin is intricately tied up in our ability to relate to God, to ourselves, and to others. Too often we make light of sin or avoid the subject because, quite frankly, facing evil can be a scary business— sort of like confronting the monster under your bed.

Confronting Evil

Sometimes, because we're afraid to confront the evil in our lives, we have an inaccurate perception of its effects on us. As a child, I was afraid of the dark and of the evil creature that I thought lived under my bed. Every night I'd switch off the light by the door, then jump the three feet from the doorway onto my bed so it couldn't reach out and grab me. Because I was afraid to look, I'd never actually seen the monster—but I knew it was there, and in my imagination it was big, bad, and ugly.

My early method of dealing with the monster under my bed was to stay as far away from it as possible, but at age twelve I decided I was too old to be afraid of the dark. *The creature under your bed is just a figment of your imagination,* I told myself. In order to conquer my fears, I decided, I had to boldly go where I had never gone before. My first daring venture was to take one step toward my bed before jumping. The next day I took two. A week later I walked to within a foot of the bed and stepped cautiously onto it.

Finally, one night as I was reading under my covers by flashlight, I decided that the only way to find out if a monster really did live under my bed was to look. I took a deep breath and switched off the flashlight. Darkness spread over me like a heavy quilt. I swallowed the fear that had lumped in my throat and inched the top half of my body over the side of the bed. With my head nearly touching the floor, I lifted the covers. When no gnarled, hairy hand reached out to grab me, I pointed the flashlight under the bed and switched it on.

I gasped—not because I saw a monster under my bed, but because I knew my mother would be furious if she saw the month's worth of clothes, crumbs, and dust that had collected there. I turned off the flashlight and went to sleep, my lips curled in a confident smile of victory.

Inside of our broken selves are dark, secret places that we often try to hide. We don't like anyone to see our dark side, and we're even more afraid to look at it ourselves. Confronting the evil inside us will not give us the same satisfaction as confronting the monster under our beds—at least not at first. When we dare to illuminate our souls and expose the evil at work in us, we won't find impotent pieces of fluff or the red-eyed monsters of our imaginations. The evil we find as we examine ourselves is far more pervasive, far more devastating than anything we can imagine.

Spiritual X rays

In order to more fully expose evil, we must be willing to fully expose ourselves. To do that we need a strong light that will penetrate our shells and illuminate our souls.

Remember Joshua, the boy with the dirt and gravel imbedded in his wounds? After cleaning Josh up, the doctor wanted to make certain he'd removed all the gravel, so he took an X ray. As he held Joshua's X ray to the light, he noticed two black spots (pebbles he had missed earlier) in Joshua's forearm. Once the pebbles were discovered, the doctor could surgically remove them.

In like manner, God provides a kind of spiritual X ray by which we can more clearly see the dirt in our souls. One of the greatest hindrances to healing is the failure to examine sin in the right light. Most of us would rather use our own dim light of self-reflection than the pure white light of God.

When you think about it, this is a natural reaction. I'd much rather have my husband see me in romantic candlelight than under glaring studio lights that expose every blemish. If and when we do allow God's penetrating light to shine through our shells and into our souls, we'll see the dark side of our nature. And perhaps, like me, you'll be surprised at what we see.

"I May Not Be Perfect, But . . ."

Sometimes we minimize the dark areas of our own souls by comparing ourselves to people whose darkness appears to be deeper and more sinister than ours. For example, if we compare ourselves to someone like Hitler, most of us look like saints.

So what if Paul has an affair with his secretary? At least he isn't robbing banks. Annette tells an occasional lie, but at least she isn't abusing her children. Sure, John and Bill use an occasional swear word and have been known to lose their tempers, but compared to the boys in the street gangs they're good kids.

Since we are created in God's image, the only one with whom we can honestly compare ourselves is God. To gain an accurate perspective of how badly broken and dirty we are, we must see ourselves next to God. When Satan can get us to look at ourselves in relation to people who appear more sinful than we are and to focus on the wrongs of others, we immediately lose sight of the dark spots in our own hearts and may eventually deny their existence.

"I'm Only Human . . ."

Another dark spot on the X ray of our souls is the place where Satan tries to convince us that doing wrong is unavoidable—that it's part of the human condition and should therefore be excused and accepted.

Sixteen-year-old Melodie had been caught shoplifting. When her parents confronted her, Melodie didn't want to talk about what she'd done. She responded not out of remorse over doing something wrong, but out of embarrassment and anger over getting caught.

After a few minutes of silence, she blurted, "Don't look at me like that. You'd think I'd committed the world's worst sin. I just messed up, okay? If you gave me more allowance I wouldn't have had to do this."

"What you did was wrong, Melodie, pure and simple," her father replied, "and you need to suffer the consequences."

It's difficult to accept ourselves as sinners. We'd rather say we "messed up," or that "we're only human." If we admit to being sinners, we must accept the fact that we might be partly to blame for our personal problems as well as for the problems of others. Many of us find evil far easier to deal with if we argue that most of the brokenness we see around us is caused by a few bad eggs.

"Nobody Said It Was a Sin . . ."

Another dark spot on our souls can be seen in our attempts to cover up sin. We devise elaborate lists by which we can gauge whether something is right or wrong. We describe sin as a list of don'ts—immoral acts, such as drinking, smoking, dancing, wearing makeup, sex, gambling, lying, stealing, anger, divorce, fornication, sexual perversion, depression, jealousy, and murder.

While reminding us that certain things are morally wrong and unhealthy for us to do, our sin list does not define all that sin entails. In fact, the list detracts from the true meaning of sin, which we'll discuss in more detail on page 53. Our lists often grow so long and detailed it becomes invalid and irrelevant.

In his book *From Sin to Wholeness* pastoral psychotherapist Dr. Brian Grant writes:

> The tragedy of this situation [defining sin as a list of don'ts] is that it invites people to poke fun at the trivialization of a life-and-death concern. We tend to forget that there are real sins, acts that truly damage self and others, and that such acts are offensive to God and to Christian conscience.[10]

"It Was Just a Little White Lie . . ."

Another issue we need to deal with regarding sin is the tendency to whitewash it. In an article called "Sin No More," Robert E. Burns writes, "Only a fool would say that sin—although, perhaps, nowhere to be seen—is not all around us, and also, in us. Part of the confusion about this, it strikes me, is that we Christians have found euphemisms, nice ways to speak of sin without naming it."[11]

Consequently, we don't *sin,* we tell "little white lies." We may be unethical, but we're not sinners. Rather than using the word "sin" to describe our immoral acts and harmful indulgences, we may use buzz words like addiction, disease, manipulative or controlling behavior, alternative lifestyles, and free choice. We relabel our vices with terms such as obsession, compulsion, misdemeanor, illness and behavior problems, or stages that we will eventually outgrow or be cured of.

Some of these terms, of course, are not necessarily synonymous with sin. In fact, many are used to diagnose legitimate physiological and psychological conditions. The problem comes when we muddle our vision by using the same terminology to cover up our sins.

The Reality of Sin

Sin then is anything that does not conform to God's will or standards. Sin is outside of God's plan for humanity. It is, according to Dr. Grant, "Whatever we do or are that *destroys,* for ourselves or another, the reality or possibility of life lived in communion with God, whether we acknowledge that fact or not. We can substitute many words for destroy—including delays, diminishes, obstructs, or dilutes. All identify acts that interfere with a person's state of peace with one's neighbor and one's self, the natural world and our Creator." Grant goes on to say that he believes "a person is happiest when that peace is achieved," and that "any sin against God also produces dislocation and unhappiness in the human realm for at least the sinner, and often for many others as well."[12]

Dr. Grant's definition surpasses the idea that sin is a specific act that marks a person as sinful and in need of judgment. For example if seventeen-year-old Allison becomes pregnant outside of marriage, our "sin list" would probably identify her as a sinner.

If we use the above definition, however, Allison's sin takes on much more serious implications than describing a solitary action. Although fornication (having sex outside of marriage) is described in the Bible as a sinful act, her pregnancy does not earmark her as evil. Rather, the sinful act is an outcome of a deeper evil presence—a root of evil that has distorted Allison's image of herself, of God, and of others. Allison hungers for fulfillment, and she made choices she hoped would give her a richer, more meaningful life. Unfortunately she used the wrong method to attain her goals. She entered into an unhealthy relationship hoping to find the answer to her dreams and instead found disappointment and pain.

Certainly, if Allison's choices had been different, she may have found a greater degree of happiness and fulfillment, but even then, because of the sin nature within her, she would be lacking. She is in part responsible for some of the pain she endures, but there is more. In Allison, we find the problem of sin that affects us all as a result of the fall. In Allison, we find feelings of inadequacy, a lack of wholeness, and a sin nature over which she has little control. This sin nature leads her to make choices that are harmful to herself and others.

Born in Sin

Scripture tells us that "sin came into the world through one man [Adam], and death through sin, and so death spread to all men because all sinned" (Rom. 5:12). Sin is like a genetic defect or curse that alters and perverts the human personality. Every human since Adam and Eve has been born in sin.

Pope Paul VI described this inbred sin as "human nature so fallen, stripped of the grace that clothed it, injured in its own natural powers and subjected to the dominion of death, that it is transmitted to all men, and it is in this sense that every man is born in sin."[13]

This is the evil nature Paul talks about in Romans 7:15: "For what I am doing I don't understand. For what I will to do, that I do not practice; but what I hate, that I do" (NKJV). Like Paul, we each have within us a destructive force—a bent toward evil that we must continually struggle against. Most of us don't want to hurt anyone, we don't want to make wrong choices or do wrong things, but we often do. For some, evil is like a raging river that sweeps them along its destructive path. Already broken and weak, they have little strength to fight back.

Dr. Grant describes this inbred sin as the "inability to love, fear of believing in one's own decisions, refusal to trust anyone, the overarching belief that life is a troublesome series of events from which no joy can be expected."[14]

We see this clearly as each generation bears a sense of shame, lack of trust, and inability to love God, one's self, and others. This troublesome life seems an endless burden from which many yearn to escape. Evil's dark, malevolent shadow hovers over us, seeking to invade us and steal our peace, joy, and our chances for fulfillment.

The effect sin has on individuals and on society is like the seepage of a chemical or toxic waste product spilled into a stream. It may have only one point of entry, but can quickly spread downstream, destroying life for miles and for decades.

Sin fouls the environment and threatens to destroy us. Evil invades our town and cities and produces a polluted atmosphere in which it is not safe for children to play or for people to walk the streets day or night. Because of humanity's bent toward sin and evil's pervasive presence, we live with the threat of nuclear war, chemical weapons, and pollution-related illnesses. Corruption widens the gap between those with power and wealth and those without. And finally, evil breeds racial unrest, apathy, distrust, fear, violence, and hatred between humans who were meant to love and cherish one another.

As we come to see how sin has invaded our lives, it helps to know that we are not alone. Everyone has fallen. Sin is any action, thought, or attitude that keeps us from being all God created us to be. It separates us from God and causes us to be unholy and broken. Consequently, all of us are sinners. The apostle Paul writes, "All have sinned and fall short of the glory of God" (Rom. 3:23). And John writes, "If we say we have no sin, we deceive ourselves, and the truth is not in us" (1 John 1:8).

Everyone craves release from suffering. Everyone is in need of healing. And we all must at some time or other let God's light penetrate us and seriously examine the dirt in our souls.

Examining the Sin in Your Life

It's time to open your journal again and read your previous definition of sin.

1. After reading this chapter, has your perception of sin changed? In what way?
2. In what way have you sinned? How have your sins affected you and others?
3. Take some time to meditate on the sinful nature in you. Ask God to penetrate your darkness with his light. Write what you see.

Examining the dark side of our souls can be depressing and discouraging. A broken egg is not a pretty sight, and probing into wounds can be painful. We've taken a long, hard look at sin and seen how invasive evil can be. We see that behind Humpty's fall and our own are not only wrong choices and actions, but faulty attitudes and even character traits. Some evil is so deeply imbedded it would take a miracle to remove it.

Humpty's condition is critical. So is ours, but hang on to your hope because in the next chapter we're going to start gathering all the fragments of our broken selves and put them back together again.

Part Two

The Healing

All the king's horses and all the king's men
Couldn't put Humpty together again.

I WONDER WHETHER HUMPTY EVER TRIED to put himself back together. It appears that he simply lay around waiting for the king's horses and men to come to his rescue. Even with his insides splattered all over the ground, you'd think he'd have done something. I certainly would have. Of course, maybe Humpty was too hurt to move.

A tragedy like that couldn't happen today, could it? Today we have super glues that can hold anything together. With our modern technology and self-help and recovery programs, we should have everything we need to pick up the pieces of our shattered lives and put ourselves, and each other, together again.

In part 2 we'll take a look at some of the glues we use to hold ourselves together, learn what we can do to help one another, and discover the secret to complete restoration.

4

Picking Up
the Pieces

DO YOU REMEMBER A TV SERIES from several years ago called "The Bionic Man"? Lee Majors played a man who had suffered multiple injuries in a fall from a plane when his parachute failed to open. A highly specialized medical team patched him up, using advanced technology to equip him with a bionic eye, an arm, and two legs.

Once they'd repaired him, he was stronger and more durable than any human. Like Superman, he could leap tall buildings in a single bound and run almost as fast as a speeding bullet.

The Bionic Egg

In the first chapter, I mentioned a retreat where the participants dropped eggs, then assessed the damage. After they'd talked about what it was like to be broken, I asked them to repair their broken eggs. If you'd like to try your hand at egg repair, gather the following supplies: a soft cloth or swatch of cotton, a spoon, some tissue, scissors, and glue. Then break an egg and follow these simple steps to put it back together again.

1. Pick out all the pieces of shell and set them aside to dry.
2. Gently put the pieces together, cradling the shell fragments in one hand or on a fluff of cotton or cloth. Reinforce cracks and open areas with glue and tissue. Leave a small opening at one end of the shell so you'll have room for the yolk and albumin.
3. Once the shell has hardened enough to be handled, scoop up as much of the white and the yolk as you can and spoon it into the opening.
4. Cap the opening with remaining shell fragments and use more tissue and glue to complete the restoration process. (To make the shell harder, more durable, and more resistant to further trauma, my more creative students have used additional layers of glue and resin to reinforce the shells and then decorated their restored eggs with clothes, arms, legs, eyes, glitter, and sequins.)

When you've completed your project, set Humpty aside to dry, then take a moment to consider the outcome. How effective was your attempt at *rehabilitating* or *re-creating* Humpty? When I asked that question of the egg-fixers at the retreat, I got some interesting responses.

Anne cradled a pieced-together Humpty in her tissue-padded hand and said, "We've put Humpty together again. I wonder why the king's horses and men couldn't manage it. He's a little strange looking and he's still seeping a bit, but by the time this last coat of glue dries, he'll be good as new—almost."

"Not really." Jenny, Anne's partner, rubbed her chin and frowned. "He's not all there. When we tried to get his insides stuffed back in we lost some. And don't forget we got some dirt in there, too."

"Don't be a pessimist, Jenny," Anne said. "He's not perfect, no one is. But with his new shell, he'll be stronger and tougher than ever. He won't be as easily hurt. I'll bet his new shell will be so strong we could drop him from a ten-foot wall and he wouldn't break."

"I don't know. He's lost part of his yolk," Kevin mused. "His cracks are still showing. His shell is rough and disfigured. He might be strong on the outside, but inside he's more vulnerable—more fragile. He's no longer on top of things. He's been separated from an important part of himself. He'll be lonely and needy and maybe feel empty inside."

"We've all been through some trauma," Anne observed. "He'll survive. Humpty has changed. So he's not the perfect specimen. He may not be all there, but he's still an egg."

"Being an eternal optimist, I can see some good coming out of this," one woman added. "I think Anne is right. Humpty's new-and-improved exterior will protect him from future falls. And that's the important thing, isn't it?"

Sam, a pastor who had been quietly observing the egg-building event said, "You know, when we first started this business I thought this Humpty Dumpty stuff was just a lot of foolishness. But we're talking about more than an egg here. The way we've created a new shell for Humpty is much like what we do to ourselves. In trying to put ourselves together we build walls and protective coverings so we can't be hurt. But the shell is a façade, created to hide our true condition. We might look okay on the outside, but inside we know the truth—we're really a poor imitation of what we were meant to be. Maybe that's why we feel guilty and unfinished so much of the time."

Putting Ourselves Together

"Nanna, would you please help me with this puzzle? It's too hard for me." Corisa, at five, knew her limitations and didn't hesitate to ask for help.

At the other end of the table, her three-year-old sister, Hannah, worked on a Bert-and-Ernie puzzle. Tight-lipped, she picked up a large piece of Bert's head and tried to squeeze it under a picnic basket. Noticing her misguided efforts, I pointed to a more likely spot and said, "Hannah, maybe it would fit better up here."

She shoved my hand away. "No, Nanna, I can do it myself!"

I admired her self-sufficiency, but she was putting the pieces in the wrong way. Her resistance to accepting help reminded me of how often we, even when we are into something far too difficult to handle, insist on doing it ourselves, in our own way.

Each of us has different ways of dealing with suffering and protecting ourselves from it. When Adam and Eve fell, they tried to hide from God. Embarrassed and ashamed, they covered themselves and pretended it hadn't happened. But God knew, of course. And when he confronted them with their sin, they blamed the serpent and one another.

Some people, like Humpty, wait for others to come along and put them together. Some, not wanting others to know they've fallen, try to take care of their own problems. They pick themselves up and hobble away to some dark corner to mend—or to die.

John tries to get on with his life, even if it means sweeping his pain under a rug and trying to forget it's ever happened.

Sam and Margaret react with anger about the injustice of it all. They sit around in large groups of similarly broken friends saying it never should have happened and ask, "Why doesn't someone do something?"

Michael and his lover carry protest signs stating that their broken condition is normal; they try to convince others and themselves that they have a right to be broken. They say brokenness is a choice—I guess they're right about that.

Our methods vary, but we've all developed thought and behavior patterns that help us adjust to, correct, or at least make sense of our messy lives. In this chapter we'll examine some self-help theories and discuss ways in which we try to manage brokenness on our own.

If It's Broken, Fix It

Whenever I see something that is broken, I try to fix it. Consequently, when I came to see the brokenness in me (low self-esteem, shame, guilt, and inadequacies), my first impulse was to fix it myself.

I was raised tough. Stoicism made me a survivor. My internal message center was filled with heroic statements such as these:

- If you want something done right, do it yourself.
- Hang in there.
- Things will get better—they sure can't get any worse.
- Don't let a little thing like depression get you down.
- Fight back.
- When life hands you lemons, make lemonade.
- Pick yourself up, dust yourself off, and start over.
- Don't let anyone see you sweat.

Survival strategies like these are part of being human and can be healthy when used appropriately. A certain amount of stoicism and resiliency can help pull us through tough times. Determination and optimism have helped me survive everything from a strong-willed child to three years of seminary. We'll do well to remember, however, that our own strength may not be enough. We'd like to pull ourselves up by our proverbial bootstraps, but we can't always get a grip.

The struggle to survive and to fix ourselves reflects the need to maintain control and a sense of balance in our lives.

Staying in Balance

Our bodies have magnificent built-in mechanisms designed to help us maintain our equilibrium, or sense of balance. When one part of the body is impaired, other parts work harder to compensate. People who have lost one of their senses such as hearing or sight find that the other senses usually compensate by becoming more highly sensitized.

When I worked as a nurse, one of my patients had lost the use of his legs as a result of a spinal-cord injury. His legs were small and limp, but his muscular upper torso had compensated for the deficiency.

My grandson Jonathan began having seizures a couple of days after he was born as a result of low blood sugar and his body's inability to properly metabolize fat. The doctor explained that seizures increase blood-sugar levels and that Jonathan's body was trying to compensate and to maintain the right balance in order to survive.

Just as our bodies struggle to maintain equilibrium, so do our minds and spirits. If something happens to disturb that balance, we will adjust and readjust ourselves to set things right, or at least compensate for the differences. This ability to recalibrate is vital to our survival. The struggle to stay in balance becomes evident at an early age when, as children, we begin to compensate for wrongs done to us.

When we are hurt or become anxious, our built-in defense mechanisms or coping skills spring into action. The moment life goes wrong, consciously or subconsciously we set out to make it right.

Defending Ourselves Against Brokenness

We use a number of defenses to keep our fragile selves together. Those defenses are similar to the glues, tissue and sequins used by the participants in my egg-repair exercise to strengthen Humpty's shell. These "glues" include the following:

- *Repression:* To put down, to force unpleasant or unbearable thoughts or memories into the unconscious.
- *Denial:* Refusing to accept a given situation.
- *Projection:* Projecting or transferring one's unacceptable thoughts, desires, and impulses onto others, thus shifting responsibility for them from ourselves to other people.
- *Rationalization:* To devise plausible and acceptable explanations for one's situation or actions, usually involving self-deceit.
- *Sublimation:* Expressing or diverting unacceptable impulses and negative energy such as inappropriate sexual desires, anxiety, anger, and fear into safe and acceptable channels.

Defense mechanisms can make us more resilient and increase our ability to cope, enabling us to handle even the most difficult problems. Unfortunately, few of us react in truly healthy ways and our defenses may, as Willard Frick, a professor and practicing psychotherapist, says, "become disruptive and self-defeating. In general, defense mechanisms distort reality and may seduce us into inaccurate perceptions and inappropriate behavior. Thus, if certain defenses become habitual and dominant in our lives, they may inhibit personal growth."[1]

As an example let's look at repression.

Repression

Jeannette, now forty, had been gang-raped at age ten. By the time she had recovered enough to walk home after the incident, she had blocked the horrifying crime from her conscious memory. Later, the issue resurfaced in the form of physical symptoms. "I suffered from severe attacks of asthma and couldn't breathe because of the pressure on my chest," Jeannette stated. "Sometimes I'd have terrible nightmares and flashbacks. I finally went to a psychiatrist who helped me go into the past (regressive therapy) to discover and face the problem. I had totally repressed it. My young mind knew that God would never let anything like that happen to a little girl. And if that were true, then it couldn't have happened. By the time I got home that night I had erased it from my conscious mind."

In a recent newspaper article, attorney and therapist Lynne Finney revealed that at age forty she underwent hypnotherapy for numerous mental and physical problems. During the course of therapy she found that she could not remember anything about the first eleven years of her childhood. Further treatment sessions revealed a painful past. She had been sexually abused and tortured by her father from ages four through eight. Finney's first reaction was denial. She felt she was going crazy. Eventually, she was able to face the trauma and work through it.

Today, Finney works with adults who were abused as children and has written a book entitled *Reach for the Rainbow*. "Our minds are incredible," Finney stated in a newspaper interview. "They protect us from what we are unable to bear. Abused children have only three choices.

They can die. They can go insane and become dysfunctional. Or they can repress it from their conscious minds until they are able to deal with it."[2]

Fortunately, most people don't experience trauma so great that they must block the memories from their conscious minds in order to survive. But most of us do use other defense mechanisms to help us cope. Many of those defenses actually worsen our condition. Instead of helping us to heal, our defenses often only cover or hide our broken selves.

The Glues We Use

In an effort to restore ourselves, we may use a number of inefficient and even toxic defenses or "glues" to patch us up and keep us functioning. Because they deal only with symptoms rather than the root problems, these "glues" usually fail. But that doesn't stop us from using them. When they start to crack or peel, we look for more potent reinforcements.

Not-me Glue

One of the most common glues is one I've termed Not-me Glue, which is made up of anger, shame, guilt, denial, betrayal, and blame. Adam and Eve used this one, shaping it into leaves to hide their nakedness.

We can use Not-me Glue to block out the truth and convince ourselves that we are fine, thank you, just fine. With a heavy enough coat we can almost convince ourselves that the cracks don't exist and that they are not a problem.

Not-me Glue makes it easy for us to blame others. We simply cover ourselves and project our inadequacies and failures onto others. If we focus hard enough on the cracks in another person's shell, we can pretend we don't have any in our own.

Anger Glue

Anger Glue comes in shades of red and is often applied liberally. Nathan wears several layers so that if anyone threatens to expose him, he flares up. He's learned that Anger Glue can keep people from coming too close.

Control Glue

Some people add a coat or two of Control Glue. This toxic substance is very effective for protecting the self and must be maintained at all costs. Kathryn uses hers as a corset, keeping her inner self tightly bound. Rob's is a fencing out-fit, complete with a sword, which he uses to keep everyone around him in line.

As-soon-as Glue

Many of us like to believe that if we could get everyone around us straightened out, our problems would melt away like a summer snow. We mix up large batches of As-soon-as Glue and set out to change the world.

As-soon-as Glue comes with a set of directions which, if followed, should lead to the peace, tranquility, and the quality of life every human desires and presumably has a right to.

Some of the As-soon-as directives for self-fulfillment are these. I'll be okay as soon as I:

- find the right mate
- lose enough weight
- earn enough money
- gain sufficient control and power
- become better organized
- find the right home, furnishings
- escape the people who drag me down

- get my spouse, children, parents, and friends to shape up
- find someone who understands me
- achieve success in the right career
- find the right doctor, treatment, or medication
- elect the right political leaders
- find the right social structure

When we use As-soon-as Glue, we can become impossibly stuck between things as they really are and dreams that can never come true. Once we are bound with this glue, we have the perfect excuse for failure. We can blame our brokenness on someone or something outside of ourselves and never need to deal with our internal damage.

If-only Paste

Sometimes when we feel insecure or inadequate we mix As-soon-as Glue with If-only Paste to make the noxious substance more potent. Martin is an If-only user. Haunted by the past, he moans relentlessly about how things might be "if only." "If only my parents had loved me," he laments. "If only I hadn't married Jane. If only I hadn't started drinking."

If only I could stop eating too much, feeling depressed, marry the right person, exercise more, change the way I live, stop feeling resentful, stop being afraid, stop feeling lonely, stop depending on others, and so on.

Busyness Resin

A lot of people I know find Busyness Resin to be a powerful anesthetic. We often deal with our brokenness and pain by filling our days with things to do, places to go, and people to see. Fran, a woman whose children have all grown up and moved away, went back to school, has a part-time job, and volunteers in three agencies. She isn't lonely or in pain. She's too busy. "The only time it hurts," Fran says, "is when I go to bed at night."

Superglue #2 with Spiritual Essence

You may be wondering how I know so much about these various glues. I know a lot of users, but to be honest, much of my knowledge comes from personal experience. Good, solid shells can hide a multitude of sins, but those of us who use them only look whole on the outside. And no matter how hard we try to pretend we're all right, an inner voice cries for attention: "Look at me! I'm still mortally wounded."

When I first discovered my own cracks and stress fractures, I used most of the glues I've mentioned, and when they didn't provide the solutions I needed, I looked for some superglue.

What I needed, I decided, was superglue topped with a couple coats of spiritual essence. Religion was the perfect glue, I reasoned. I applied a thick layer over my cracked self and lavishly sprinkled on glitter so that everyone could see my spiritual glow. The strategy was simple: I'd go to church, play the part of a happy homemaker, and imagine I was right with God and with the world.

I'd heard that if you acted the part on the outside, the inside would eventually conform. So, with just the right amount of glue and glitter, I placed myself and my family among the other spiritual families and consistently occupied the fifth pew from the back.

Every Sunday we dressed in our best clothes, and after a few tears, arguments, and agonizing over my family's snail-like pace, we'd be off. We looked great—the all-American family.

I learned a lot about keeping up appearances in church. For one thing, if you want everyone to see you as a spiritual family, never let your children sit together. Put an adult between them so they can't blow your cover by getting into a brawl.

One Sunday morning, just about the time I had begun to feel secure, my superglue with Spiritual Essence cracked. Our perfect family image crumbled as I sat in the pew of our church and glanced at my ten-year-old son. Shock ricocheted through my body. How could I have missed it? He'd looked perfect when we left the house. But now, from under his neatly pressed suit pants peeked the ragged hem of an old pair of jeans, and below that (gasp!), his old ragged tennis shoes. Tucked under his white shirt and tie I could make out the plaid of an old, frayed flannel shirt.

"Why?" I asked him when we left the church and were out of earshot of the other worshipers. "How could you do this to me?"

He shrugged and turned up the corners of his mouth in an impish grin. "Superman does it. Besides, I wanted to be ready to play faster when we get to Grandma's house at the farm."

Great, I thought to myself. *He's playing Superman and my reputation is ruined.*

Oh, it wasn't just the clothes—that I could have handled. David had inadvertently broken through my defenses. My fear was not that my son be seen wearing grungy sneakers, but that someone might see through the façade I'd worked so hard to create.

The Glues You Use

You've read about various ways in which we try to mend our broken selves, and now I'd like you to think about your line of defenses and the attempts you've made to put yourself together again.

1. Have you suppressed or repressed memories of the past? (If portions of your life seem blocked out and you suspect you may have been abused, you may want to see a counselor or psychotherapist to help you deal with it. In the next chapter I'll address getting professional help.)
2. Have you handled the hurts in your life by using, in healthy ways, the various defense mechanisms I've mentioned or have you used unhealthy glues and resins to cover up? List the methods you may have used to hold yourself together and evaluate their effectiveness.
3. Take a few minutes to listen to your inner voice. Is it saying, "I am well, healed, and perfect"? Or is it saying, "Help me. I might look put together on the outside, but inside I'm still broken"?

Sometimes our defenses help us to get through difficult times, but sooner or later we must face the reality that our do-it-yourself attempts are like applying a bandage to a gaping wound. Regardless of how good we are at applying glues and rebuilding our broken shells, our efforts will never be good enough to bring complete healing. For that, we need help.

5

All the King's Men
—and Women

THOSE OF US WHO STRUGGLE to put ourselves together again discover all too soon that the end results aren't always what we'd like them to be. We may become functional, but inside we still struggle with disharmony, losses, and a sense that something isn't quite right. Pieces are still missing or misplaced.

In the last chapter I mentioned that my grandson Jonathan experienced some serious health problems shortly after his birth. After several weeks of tests, the doctors determined that he had a rare metabolic disorder. Jonathan's body did what it could to help him survive, but he needed help. Without medical intervention Jonathan would have died.

At times we, too, may find ourselves in critical condition emotionally and spiritually. In the last chapter I mentioned my own ineffective attempts at self-healing. Eventually I came to realize that I couldn't handle my brokenness alone. I, like Jonathan, needed help to survive.

Getting Help

Clinical depression had tied me up and thrown me into a helpless, hopeless heap. I look back at that time in my life with awe and a sense of wonder. Even though I was totally devastated, my "fall" became a turning point that set me on the path to wholeness and healing. And that healing began as I laid aside my pride and fears and asked for help.

"What's the matter?" Sharon, my supervisor, asked when she found me in the nurses' lounge.

I wiped the tears from my face and lifted my head to look at her, but all I could see was a white blur. I'd fallen apart for the third time that morning. "I . . . don't know," I stammered. "I can't seem to stop crying." I sniffed and reached for another tissue.

"I know taking care of Mr. Allen is tough, Pat. Would it help to talk?"

"It's not Mr. A." I was dealing okay with his stroke. The likeable older patient was dying, but the grief attacking me that morning was from something else—something I couldn't place. "I just don't understand. I've never felt this down before." I dabbed at my eyes, trying not to smear my makeup. Not that it mattered, since my eyes were already red and puffy from my cry during the drive into work that morning. "I just feel so overwhelmed." Panic rose in my throat and I swallowed to hold it back. "I'm so scared."

"Is it Ron?" she asked. "Or one of the kids?"

I shook my head. "No, they're fine. It's me. I think I'm going crazy. I just don't know what to do."

Sharon reached for the phone. "I'll call for a replacement. You're going to see your doctor."

"But . . ."

"No buts. Just go."

My supervisor saw my need, took charge, and sent me into the arms of people who helped me make it through my "dark night of the soul." Sharon, though she didn't actually put me together herself, encouraged me to seek the help I needed.

Sharon convinced me that I needed help to deal with my broken life, and I went to see my doctor. When I'd finished telling him how I felt, he placed a hand on my shoulder and said, "It sounds like you could use a rest."

I nodded.

"I'm not a psychologist, but I'd say you are probably suffering from acute depression."

I wanted to argue but didn't. Instead I buried my head in my hands and wondered how it could have happened. A few moments later I heard him say ". . . hospital," and realized I hadn't been listening.

"What?" I mumbled.

"I said, I think we'd better put you in the hospital for a few days. They have a mental ward and I'll transfer you over to a psychiatrist there."

The words "mental ward" and "psychiatrist" screamed through my head like sirens. *No!* I wanted to cry. *I can't go! I'll be okay. Please don't send me to a hospital! I don't belong there.* But I didn't argue. I knew in my heart that he was right.

Giving myself permission to accept help was difficult. As I look back, I'm thankful I didn't resist. My doctor's plan to pull me from the wreckage my life had become helped— almost immediately. With no demands—no meals to fix, clothes to wash, or husband, kids, or patients to care for— I began to relax.

The nurses injected me with tranquilizers to help me cope with the pain and gave me pills to lift my spirits. I also began to attend group sessions where I could relate to other broken people.

My psychiatrist, who wore a three-piece suit and a caring expression, listened while I told him about my fall. We talked about the reasons I'd fallen, and he helped me find ways to avoid depression and handle stress in the future.

Did the intervention and therapy help? Can the king's men and women really succeed in putting the Humpties of the world back together again? In part, yes. In my case, psychotherapy helped me through a difficult time. It gave me enough strength to survive until I could find a permanent solution.

I'll discuss that solution in the next chapter, but first let's take a closer look at the way in which we can help one another in the healing process.

We Need One Another

The first step toward healing is to recognize that we are indeed broken people. The second step is to realize we can't heal ourselves. The third and perhaps most difficult step is to admit our need for help.

In Genesis 2:18, God declared that it was not good for the human to be alone in the world. God recognized our need for intimacy and companionship with others like ourselves. That not only means enjoying one another's company, it means we are to be available to one another in times of trouble and help meet one another's needs.

Hebrews 10:24 and 25 states, "And let us consider one another in order to stir up love and good works, . . . exhorting [encouraging] one another" (NKJV). And the apostle Paul says we are to bear one another's burdens (Gal. 6:2).

Most of us understand the importance of helping others in times of crisis. We offer help to the woman who recently lost her husband; we give support to those suffering through divorce; we offer an empathetic heart and comforting shoulder to the cancer patient. Whatever the problem, most of us are ready to offer help and encouragement to lighten their burdens.

However, we are not always comfortable in our care-giving. We tend to avoid pain and don't like being around people who are suffering. Thus, we often put up invisible barriers to keep ourselves from getting too close or too involved. These walls send signals like, "I'll sit with you a spell and have coffee and talk about the weather, but don't tell me that you're dying, or how much you hurt, because I'll have to leave." Sadly, few people are trained to listen well or demonstrate empathy and compassion.

On the other side, barriers may be even higher and stronger. As difficult as it may be to help others, it is even harder for some people to admit the need for help, and more difficult still to ask for it. My church has a lay-care-giving program called Stephen Series, in which Stephen Ministers are trained to listen to, encourage, and assist hurting people.

As a leader in this caring ministry, I'm continually amazed at the number of wounded people who decline offers of help, saying, "I'm fine. Really, I'll be okay. I don't need anyone."

We often feel uncomfortable when others offer their assistance. We hate for people to see our helplessness, and we don't want to be a burden. When we hurt, we often want to keep it to ourselves. Stubborn pride, fear of exposure, and fear of what others may think prevent us from asking for help.

It is important to remember that although we are called to be caregivers when others are hurting, we are also called to be care-receivers when our own lives are in pieces. Psychologist Scott Peck writes:

> Trapped in our tradition of rugged individualism, we are extraordinarily lonely people. . . . Look at the sad, frozen faces all around you and search in vain for the souls hidden behind masks of make-up, masks of pretense, masks of composure. . . . We are desperately in need of a new ethic of "soft individualism," an understanding of individualism

which teaches that we cannot be truly ourselves until we are able to share freely the things we most have in common: our weaknesses, our incompleteness, our imperfection, our inadequacy, our sins, our lack of wholeness and self-sufficiency. . . . It is a kind of softness that allows those necessary barriers, or outlines, of our individual selves to be like permeable membranes, permitting ourselves to seep out and the selves of others to seep in.[1]

Allowing others to help us when we fall is a vital step to becoming whole again. But once we admit we need help, we face more questions: Where do I go for help? Do I simply confide in a friend, or do I need professional help? Who can I trust?

Where Do I Go for Help?

My bout with depression called for drastic measures. I needed to escape the treadmill my life had become: I needed professional help.

Don, who is struggling through a divorce, has found that a support group helps him cope. Mary, on the other hand, was advised by several friends to seek counseling to help her work through her child's death. Ken, an alcoholic who is unable to stop drinking, has taken his pastor's advice and entered a drug-and-alcohol-treatment program. Fran and Bill, a couple who have found themselves in serious financial trouble, have opted to go to a financial counselor.

Adrianne's husband has Alzheimer's disease. She is getting emotional support from her Stephen Minister as well as from a support group for families of Alzheimer patients.

You may be wondering how to find help. Ask. Seek advice from friends who have had similar experiences, ask a pastor, or make an appointment with a counselor.

As you can see, many options are available. It's important to remember, however, that mental health is not an exact science. There are as many philosophies on what's best for the human psyche as there are therapists. Unfortunately, the field of psychology has its share of charlatans. If you decide to seek professional help, be careful. Take time to determine whether the program, support group, or individual counselor you choose is right for you.

What do you look for? Basically, people who care. Research seems consistently to find empathy, warmth, and genuineness characteristic of human encounters that change people for the better.[2]

Before you enter therapy, you'll want to find out whether the therapist meets the following criteria:

- Has a value system and philosophy of life that is compatible with yours. (If you are a Christian, you may want a Christian counselor.)
- Can identify with your particular concerns.
- Will answer your questions and keep you informed as to the type of therapy used, the rationale behind it, and the progress you make.
- Can understand and relate to your particular background and culture.

It is also a good idea to evaluate your counseling experience from time to time. Ask yourself these questions: Is therapy really helping? Why am I going? How is the program changing my life? How am I getting better?

We All Need Support

We do not all need professional counseling, but we all need support. Some of today's most popular counseling programs are those that include support groups. Support systems in which we can be honest about our brokenness and pain and find encouragement are essential to our emotional well-being. Support systems come in a variety of forms: friends getting together to sew quilts, have lunch, or just chat; a weekend retreat; a phone call; a hug. Support can also be found in a formal support or recovery group in which persons with similar struggles help one another through difficult times. Important elements of a support system are a healthy environment, education, and empowerment.

A Safe Environment

For emotional health we need a safe place, somewhere we can go to confess our hurts, our needs, and our sins. I have several such safe places. One is a prayer group where participants are able to freely express their needs and receive comfort, support, and prayer. No matter what I say to my friends, I know they will still love and respect me. What freedom there is in being able to call a friend and say, "I'm in trouble" or "I'm hurting." I appreciate having people I can call when I'm suffering, and I like being available to others.

When counselors, whether friends or professionals, show caring concern and empathy and are genuine in the relationship, they create a safe place in which we can explore our problems and work on solutions. Confidentiality and trust are vital to this type of relationship.

Education

Education is another important part of the healing process. Knowledge and understanding are necessary to becoming whole. Many self-help books, seminars, and classes are available to help us discover why we are broken and learn what we can do about it. We can learn how to avoid and/or deal with some of the problems we encounter and how to replace faulty attitudes and belief systems with healthy ones. Education can also help us improve relationships and methods of communication.

As with counselors and psychological theories, not all types of education are right for everyone. Healthy education involves an effort to read and study widely and search for truth so that we are not easily deceived by people who say they have the answer but in the end offer only false hope.

Empowerment

One of the most therapeutic approaches is empowering broken people—helping them to cope with life's obstacles so they can make significant, positive changes in their lives. Empowerment comes as we work through our problems with a positive, yet honest, approach to finding solutions and methods of coping. We do well to take the apostle Paul's advice and think about what is good, right, positive, and possible in our world, rather than dwelling on what is wrong and impossible (see Phil. 4:8).

This positive-thinking approach works well as long as we use it to help us deal with problems and not simply use it as a defense to help us avoid pain or to convince ourselves that problems don't exist. Focusing on what we can do empowers us to find solutions. Acquiring tools to face the truth about life and its troubles can help us to overcome adversity.

For example, ten-year-old Robbie couldn't sleep at night. His father had abused him, and in a counseling session Robbie said, "I dreamed that my dad came into my room through the window and killed me. He could do it for real."

After empathizing with his fears, I said, "I wonder what could protect you so you wouldn't have to be afraid anymore."

Robbie thought for a moment. His eyes widened and a smile emerged. "A dragon! If I had a dragon outside my room he'd make sure I was safe."

"Could you have a dragon?"

"Sure, he's in my 'magination. He's mean and a hundred feet high."

"Oh, he sounds scary."

"He is, but don't worry," Robbie assured me. "He won't hurt you, 'cause you helped make him."

Robbie had no trouble sleeping in his room after that. To an adult, this may seem like a childish game, but for Robbie, a guard dragon was exactly what he needed to help him cope with his nightmares.

In recent years, I have learned to tap into my God-given strength. I don't imagine dragons, but I do imagine myself being held and cared for by God. God is far more powerful than any fear. When I'm experiencing an especially difficult time, I envision God holding me safely in his arms. I see God's love as a shield around me to protect me from all harm.

The dragon empowered Robbie to overcome his fears. God empowers me. We'll learn more about God and his power supply in the next chapter, but now I'd like to focus on another aspect that should be part of the help we give and get from others.

Others Can Help, but They Can't Heal

Friends and professional counselors can lend us a hand, carry us through hard times, and make our burdens easier to bear. Many skilled and competent counselors and helpful recovery or support groups are available to help us get ourselves back together.

We have sophisticated programs available to us that help us to deal with our problems, understand ourselves, and promote healing. We can come out of our recovery experience as functional beings. We can learn to live with our cracks and fractures and to be content with our imperfect selves. We convince ourselves we're okay just the way we are—that we are, in fact, normal. And we are. It's normal to sin. It's normal to be broken. But is normalcy enough?

Scripture tells us it is not. The apostle Paul says in his letter to the Romans, "Do not be conformed to this world, but be *transformed* by the renewing of your mind, that you may prove what is that good and acceptable and perfect will of God" (Rom. 12:2 NKJV, emphasis added).

We are not to be conformed to the worldly pattern where immoral behavior and attitudes are so prevalent that they are considered normal. Rather we are to be transformed so that we reflect the image of God, not the image of broken humanity. To be broken and to make the best of it is normal. But why should we settle for the norm when God offers us so much more?

Before moving on to the next chapter where we'll read about God's ultimate plan for health and wholeness, pull out your journal and make a few entries about your emotional state.

1. Brokenness effects us emotionally. How is your emotional health? Do you need help?
2. Do you have friends and/or a support group where you can talk about your fears, concerns, and problems?
3. If you have had counseling, how did it help you?
4. Have you found complete healing, or is there still a part of you that feels broken?

The writer of the Humpty story was right—all the king's horses and all the king's men couldn't put Humpty together again. If we are honest with ourselves, we'll admit that no matter how effective our efforts and the efforts of others may be, they cannot bring about total health, healing, and wholeness. In the end, though we can put the pieces of a broken shell back together and secure it with layers of fabric, tissue, and glue, all we have to show for our efforts is a patched shell that houses a broken soul.

We are limited in what we can do and in the changes we can bring about. As a counselor, I've often been frustrated that I couldn't make more of a difference, that I didn't have some kind of magic formula or sage advice that would turn my clients' lives around.

During my training as a Stephen Minister and again in my graduate work in counseling, when I began to expect too much of people and of myself I would remember what Ken Haugk, clinical psychologist and founder of the Stephen Series, says: "We are caregivers, not cure-givers." We can love and care for people, we can walk alongside them and give support, we can pray and offer encouragement, but the curing lies in God's hands and in their own response to God's offer to heal us and make us whole.

Only God

In part 1 we saw how evil and resulting sin caused our brokenness. It alienated us from God and locked us into the bondage of loneliness and isolation. It destroyed our ability to relate to one another without the need to protect ourselves through control, domination, and manipulation. And worse, it caused a darkness to cover our inner eyes and distort the image of God in us.

The power to remove the dirt from our souls and repair the damage requires a strength we do not have. Evil reigns on a spiritual level and must be fought by spiritual means. We can be partners with God in the process, but only God has the ability to heal a broken yolk. Only God can restore a godly image in us. And only God can re-create our broken souls so that we can be whole (holy) once more.

So let your prayer be as the psalmist's when he sings:

> Create in me a clean heart, O God,
>   and put a new and right spirit within me.
> Cast me not away from thy presence,
>   and take not thy holy Spirit from me.
> Restore to me the joy of thy salvation,
>   and uphold me with a willing spirit.

> Psalm 51:10–12 RSV

6

Restoring
the Soul

THE WRITER OF THE HUMPTY DUMPTY RHYME did a terrible thing. He or she let evil win. To allow evil to triumph over good is immoral. My soul cries out for justice, and I must satisfy a deep need to rewrite the ending.

Humpty Dumpty: The Revised Version

Humpty has fallen. All attempts to repair the broken egg have failed. Unless we find a savior for Humpty, he will remain broken for eternity. Will no one rescue him? Hopelessness casts darkness over the scene.

A golden-haired egg in a transparent shell appears on the horizon. Princess Grace, the king's only daughter, approaches the small gathering of mourners.

"Why are you crying?" she asks.

"It's Humpty," one of the men sobs. "We've tried and tried, but we can't put him together."

Grace falls to her knees and gathers the broken egg in her arms. "There is only one way to save him," she said sadly. "We must each give Humpty a part of our yolk."

They gasp and back away. "But that could kill us," they murmur. "Better to have one die than for all of us to suffer."

The princess sighs. "Very well. I cannot force you. I alone will give him the yolk he needs."

The other eggs object, but since she is royalty, they finally give in. Part of her yolk is transplanted into Humpty: Grace flows into Humpty and fills him. The sacrifice weakens Grace, and for a time the eggs think she has died. Then something strange happens. The portion of yolk still left inside her begins to grow and she becomes stronger and more radiant than ever.

Humpty Dumpty, full of Grace, begins his ascension to the top of the wall, where he marries the princess and lives happily ever after.

In Need of a Hero

Like Humpty, we too were in need of someone to save us—someone to rescue us from our broken and sinful state. At this point, if you are a Christian, you may be able to say, "I've already found a Savior. Christ has rescued me."

You may have accepted Christ as your Savior and have been filled with God's grace. And, like Humpty, you may be living happily, basking in the joy of your salvation. Or, you may not.

Sadly, many Christians have accepted Christ, yet still feel broken and unfinished. They believe God has saved them, or want to believe, yet somehow the rescue doesn't seem real. It may be ingrained in the mind, but not in the heart. The Bible says we should be walking in the light, yet for the most part they are still lying in the pits of darkness, hoping for a hero.

Over the years our imaginations have created all types of superheroes—mystical, magical, and otherworldly characters, who transcend their human woes and find happy-ever-afters: Superman, Wonder Woman, Spiderman, and

Batman; Cinderella and Snow White and their Prince Charmings; Beauty and the Beast; and, of course, the Little Mermaid who loved her human so much she risked her life in order to save him.

Our fairy-tale heroes give us dreams of castles in the air, of being rescued, redeemed, and made new. They restore hope that perhaps we can rise above our circumstances, no matter how difficult. We look to heroes as models after whom we can pattern our lives, and we look to them for answers to guide us out of our despair into a world where we, too, can capture villains, slay dragons, and overcome evil.

Did you ever wonder where our ability to create heroes comes from? With any imagination at all, we can create princes who slay dragons and restore peace out of chaos. I suspect our heroes come out of an inner knowledge that there really is a supreme being who can save us. Our imaginings are the soul's way of guiding us to a truth that proclaims a higher quality of life and a savior, who can, through a pure heart and superior strength, defeat our enemies and restore us to perfection.

The good-prevails-over-evil motif was in place long before Steven Spielberg created Indiana Jones. Many of our fictional characters are based on biblical principles and godly people. Over and over in the Old Testament God sent heroes to rescue his people and deliver them out of the hands of their enemies. In fact, the story began about the time of the great fall and is still being played out in the hearts of individuals today. We get into trouble and God reaches out with an offer of help.

The Original Story

In chapter 2 of Genesis we saw how God lovingly created humankind. We saw also the devastating effects of the fall, when our world was shattered and we lost our perfect relationship with God. Adam and Eve changed from being *wholly* human (holy and complete) to being *only* human.

All of our efforts, while valiant and often commendable, have succeeded only in making us somewhat functional. Yet God loves us far too much to allow us to remain broken. God, knowing our weaknesses and inability to save ourselves, designed a way to give us back the life we'd lost in the fall. As a parent I can understand that love.

When our son crashed into adolescence, he made a number of damaging choices—including running away from home. My husband and I tried everything to turn him around. Finally, when he'd run out of options he called us.

We told him to come home and we'd talk. The first thing we did was to tell him we loved him and wanted to help but that we couldn't allow him to continue living the way he had been. Then we asked if he'd be willing to make some changes. He agreed and changed the course of his life.

God gives us a chance to come home as well.

A Second Chance

"For God so loved the world that He gave His only begotten Son, that whoever *believes* in Him should not perish but have everlasting life. For God did not send His Son into the world to condemn the world, but that the world through Him might be saved" (John 3:16–17 NKJV, emphasis added).

God took a part of his being, planted himself in a woman's womb, and became one of us. In Christ, God took on human form and became the second Adam. This time the outcome was different. Christ resisted temptation. He faced off against the evil one and won the battle for our souls.

As scholar and theologian Charles Carter writes, "The sullying of humanity's *imago Dei* [divine image] through the Fall made necessary the renewed, perfect *imago Dei* in the God-man, Christ Jesus, in order that humanity might be restored to God and His original image might be restored in humankind."[1]

Jesus returned us to God and reinstated the freedom we lost in the fall. In Christ, we can once more be identified with God and be in harmonious and intimate relationship with him. When we are reunited with God, we find our true identities and the missing part of our inner selves. We are cleansed, purified, and made whole. The emptiness inside of us is filled with God's grace. The darkness of our souls is cleansed by God's pure love.

As restored humans, we are once more able to love God with all of our hearts, souls, and minds, and our neighbors as ourselves. And in our holiness (wholeness) we can again reflect God's glory. Once more, we are truly human and, as God's representatives, God's purpose can be accomplished through us.

Just Believe

God wrote a happy ending to our once tragic story. God gave us a Savior, "the Lamb of God who takes away the sin of the world!" (John 1:29 NKJV). Believe this, the Bible assures us, and we will be saved. But what if we have doubts?

In *A Circle of Quiet,* Madeleine L'Engle writes about a seminar for high school students in which a fifteen-year-old student asked: "Do you really believe in God with no doubts at all?"

Madeleine answered, "I really and truly believe in God, with all kinds of doubts. But I base my life on this belief."[2]

It's difficult for most of us to honestly and totally, without reservation, say, "I believe." We may want to. We try to convince ourselves it's true. Yet even the most dedicated Christians sometimes struggle to maintain their faith.

If I'm tied to a railroad track and a train is racing toward me, I have no trouble believing I'm going to die. I can look at a chair and believe it's there. I believe in rational and tangible things because they are a part of my reality.

We can't see God. We can't scientifically measure or prove his existence. God's presence in our lives is often overshadowed by doubt and the present reality of our pain. For many adults, the promise of being saved and living forever seems impossible.

The kind of belief we need is that of a child. I'm reminded of a story I read recently about a little girl who was coloring a picture. "What are you making?" her mother asked.

"I'm drawing a picture of God," the girl replied.

Her mother smiled. "But no one knows what God looks like."

The girl gave her mother a knowing smile and said, "They will when I'm done drawing him."

As children, many of us had no problem believing in God. In chapter 12 we'll examine how to regain some of those childlike characteristics. Born without shells, children are soft and transparent. Unfortunately, as we grow older, the ability to believe disappears under layers of disillusionment, cynicism, and doubt. Yet there is still a part of us that wants to believe. The child in us may still be drawing a picture of God, but our adult minds refuse to see him clearly and resist the image.

Doubt, according to Paul DeVries, professor of philosophy at Wheaton College (Ill.), "is necessary to sustain the vitality of the Christian walk." He maintains there is a difference between doubt and unbelief.

> Doubt is the act of questioning, the expression of uncertainty. Doubt is the humility of a mind asking real questions and seeking real solutions. Surely one can believe and question at the same time. In fact, if we did not believe, we would not question. . . . unbelief, [on the other hand] connotes stubborn resistance, disobedience, and rebellion. In short, doubt is the sincere question, but unbelief is the willingness to hear the answer.[3]

We need the freedom, as does a child, to come to God with everything we are feeling. As De Vries says, ". . . if I do not sincerely express my doubts to God in the frequent pain and disappointments of my life, how can I say that I believe he is all-loving, all-knowing, and all powerful?"[4]

"We see through a glass, darkly" (1 Cor. 13:12). Our lenses and shells are dirtied by sin and denial, but we can daily offer them to God for cleaning. We may know only in part, but we can ask God to show us more. We can yearn for answers and hunger for that time when we will see God face to face, when we will fully understand God as he fully understands us.[5]

God understands our doubts and works in us to give us the faith we lack. Scripture reminds us that even in our doubts there is hope. The Gospel of Mark tells the story of a man who came to Jesus hoping Jesus could heal his son, who suffered from seizures.

> "Teacher, I brought You my son, who has a mute spirit. And wherever it seizes him, it throws him down; he foams at the mouth, gnashes his teeth, and becomes rigid. So I spoke to Your disciples, that they should cast it out, but they could not."
>
> He answered him and said, "O faithless generation, how long shall I be with you? How long shall I bear with you? Bring him to Me."
>
> [The man came, and after answering Jesus' questions about the boy's illness, said] ". . . if you can do anything, have compassion on us and help us."
>
> Jesus said to him, "If you can believe, all things are possible to him who believes."
>
> Immediately the father of the child cried out . . . , "Lord I believe; help my unbelief!"
>
> Mark 9:17–24 NKJV, emphasis added

Jesus healed the boy despite the father's doubts and later reassured the disciples who had failed to heal him.

After Jesus had risen, it took an empty tomb and several personal appearances before his disciples believed. When the women who were the first to hear the news told

the other disciples, everyone thought they were crazy
except Peter, who ran to see for himself (Luke 24:1–12).

In his final visit with the disciples, Jesus appeared to
them and "they were terrified," thinking they'd seen a
ghost. Jesus calmed them, saying, "Why are you troubled?
And why do doubts arise in your hearts? Behold My hands
and My feet, that it is I Myself. Handle Me and see, for a
spirit does not have flesh and bones as you see I have"
(Luke 24:38–39 NKJV).

What we lack in faith God will provide. We may not be
able to see all that God has done because we are straining
to see through the thick, heavy shells we've built around
ourselves. Our vision might also be impaired because we
are still experiencing the pain of being broken.

Phantom Pains

In a sense we are like Michael, whose leg was smashed
in a motorcycle accident. He suffered excruciating pain for
months while doctors tried to restore his leg. Finally, when
all efforts to save it failed, they amputated it. Michael's pain
should have stopped, but it didn't. Months later, a phantom pain still remained in the leg that was no longer there.

Christ has healed our broken spirits and has won the
battle over evil, but perhaps because we have suffered so
long—perhaps because we feel the phantom pains, or are
blinded by our shells—we can't quite accept the healing as
real. Thus we go on living as though Christ's work was
never done.

Part of Michael's healing will be to accept the fact that
the act is done and to go on living as though he is healed,
regardless of the way he feels. The pain eventually sub-
sided for Michael, and it can for us as well.

Telling Ourselves the Truth

Despite what our feelings and phantom pains tell us,
Christ has saved and restored us. The key to accepting the

gift is trusting the giver and believing not necessarily in what we feel, but in what God tells us in his Word. We guard ourselves against Satan's lies by asking God to wrap us in truth.

Our salvation comes as we acknowledge our brokenness, accept Jesus Christ as our Savior, and live believing that we have been restored.

Perhaps you have had difficulty accepting God's gift of grace and restoration. Take a moment and write about your doubts and confusion in your journal. Christ has healed your soul, washed away all the dirt and grime imbedded there, taken you out of the hands of the evil one, and restored you to God. But perhaps like Michael you still feel the phantom pains of brokenness within you.

Some of you may already be Christians, yet still suffer these phantom pains. Even so, be encouraged, for as the Bible says, God ". . . has begun a good work in you and will complete it . . ." (Phil. 1:6 NKJV). The healing is happening. Since it is a process it doesn't happen all at once as we'll see in the next few chapters.

If you're still feeling broken the following Bible verses and commentary may reassure you. Think about them, study them, and write your responses to them in your journal.

1. "Most assuredly, I say to you [one] who hears My word and believes in Him who sent Me has everlasting life, and shall not come into judgment, but has passed from death into life" (John 5:24 NKJV). The moment you believe, you are saved and given everlasting life. Do you want to believe that Jesus has saved you?

2. "And you, who were once alienated and enemies in your mind by wicked works, yet now He has reconciled in the body of his flesh through death, to present you holy and blameless, and irreproachable in His sight" (Col. 1:21–22 NKJV).

Once reconciled, we are without blemish and free from accusation. Christ transforms us from aliens (people with false and broken images of themselves) to holy, blameless, and acceptable persons in whom God's Spirit can now dwell.

Reconciliation is recorded in the Bible as a fact—an event that has already taken place. When reconciliation is discussed, it is God who reconciles us to himself. He performs the action on us, but never on himself because there is no need for him to change. He is the same—forever. The act has been accomplished. Do you want to believe that?

3. "Be reconciled to God" (2 Cor. 5:20 NKJV). As we've discussed, reconciliation is a gift. If the work is to be accomplished in us, we need to accept that gift and thus be restored to wholeness. This verse is written as a command. Paul is imploring, pleading with us to take what God has so graciously offered. Can you do that?

To not be reconciled to God means to continue living in alienation and wickedness. When we are alienated from him, we are strangers to and enemies of God, and we belong to the evil one. Unlike Adam and Eve, we've seen the consequences of a world caught in the intricate and deadly web of sin. Had they known the damage their disobedience would cause, they may have responded differently. As we stand in the space between life and death, we are confronted with two choices: We can ask forgiveness, raise our arms to God and be reconciled with our heavenly Father, becoming holy and blameless and looking forward to eternal life, or we can die. We can remain in the dark where we continue to be strangers [enemies] to God, belonging to another [Satan], being wicked, hostile— doomed to eternal death.

A Leap of Faith

The restoration is an intangible thing. Søren Kierkegaard, an existentialist philosopher, stated that we, in our human understanding and experience, cannot prove God's existence. To believe in God and what God has done demands that we go beyond our minds into our souls and take a "leap of faith."

That leap is not so difficult when we consider the alternatives. Madeleine L'Engle put it this way:

> There are three ways you can live life. . . . You can live life as though it's all a cosmic accident; we're nothing but an irritating skin disease on the face of the earth. Maybe you can live your life as though everything's a bad joke. I can't. . . .
>
> Or you can go out at night and look at the stars and think, yes, they were created by a prime mover, and so were you, but he's aloof perfection, impassible, indifferent to his creation. He doesn't care, he only cares about the ultimate end. . . . You don't matter to him, I don't matter to him, except possibly as a means to an end. I can't live that way either. . . .
>
> Then there's a third way: to live as though you believe that the power behind the universe is a power of love, a personal power of love, a love so great that all of us really do matter to him. He loves us so much that every single one of our lives has meaning; he really does know about the fall of every sparrow, and the hairs of our head are really counted. That's the only way I can live.[6]

I too, must believe that God is a God of love and compassion, who cares for and saves us. The Bible attests to this sort of God, and my spirit does also.

Holy Glue

> *"Man is born broken; he lives by mending. The grace of God is the glue."*
>
> Eugene O'Neill

God's love and grace are unconditional. They are a kind of holy glue God offers to everyone. Our own glues and those others used to patch us together are limiting. The shells we patch, though effective for a time, will not last forever. God's holy glue is eternal. It is a hiding place (Ps. 32:7), a shelter (Ps. 61:4), a refuge and fortress (Ps. 31:2), in which we can feel safe from the storms that wash over us and the falls that threaten to destroy us. Here in God's embrace, we can begin to discover wholeness as a reality rather than an impossible dream.

Part Three

Living a Whole (Holy) Life

YEARS AGO IN ITALY, A YOUNG ARTIST SCULPTED AN ANGEL and then hid himself so he could hear what the master, Michelangelo, would say about the work.

The master examined the statue while the young artist breathlessly looked on. After a time, he heard Michelangelo say, "It lacks only one thing."

The brokenhearted artist couldn't eat or sleep wondering what he had done wrong. Concerned, a friend went to the master and asked what the statue lacked. Michelangelo said, "It lacks only life; if it had life, it would be as perfect as God Himself could make it."[1]

Sometimes in our attempts to heal or re-create ourselves, we lack the one thing vital to our existence—life. We breathe the air our physical bodies need to survive, but inside, spiritually, we are often as lifeless as a statue because we have not given up our shells and allowed the breath of God to awaken us.

We may acknowledge God and perhaps even feel a degree of safety in the shelter he provides, but being made whole entails much more than acceptance of God's grace and love—his Holy Glue. In order to fully experience life, we must allow God to penetrate our innermost being. We must open ourselves to receive his Holy Spirit and give God permission to change us.

God sent his Son to restore us and free us from sin. We are free, as were Adam and Eve prior to the fall, to enter into an intimate relationship with God. He also sent his Holy Spirit, to renew and restore us from the inside out. When we open ourselves, the Spirit enters us like a wind and permeates our bodies, minds, and spirits. God breathes into us new life.

In this phase of the restoration process, we join with God to re-create ourselves more fully in God's image. This does not happen instantly, but is a process that can take years, perhaps even a lifetime. God's redemptive work, of course, is immediate; ours is not. The time re-creation takes depends on how quickly we are able to change or let go of our old attitudes, belief systems, habits, and shells.

We'll begin the process by first identifying these attitudes and beliefs that hinder the healing process and keep us from being one with God.

1

Going Back
to the Garden

"You are a sinner! Repent and believe!"

"Christ died to set you free!"

"Trust God! Have faith!"

"God is the answer to all your problems! All you have to do to be saved is to ask Jesus into your heart!"

These shouts came from two young men on a street corner in Honolulu who were handing out gospel tracts. Even though there was truth in what they were saying, I found myself wanting to argue, *"It isn't that simple."*

In a way it angered me to see the gospel message handed out in much the same way charlatans would sell bottles of magic potions that could supposedly cure anything from a sore throat to impotence—a quick fix, an instant cure.

I've been a Christian nearly all my life and have seen a lot of people who have said "yes" to Jesus and who are elated to have finally found "the answer." Then weeks, months, or years later they turn away disillusioned because things aren't going according to plan. In their disappointment they ask difficult questions:

- If God is the answer and he really has sent Jesus to rescue me, why am I still broken?
- If I am restored and perfected in Christ like the Bible says, why am I still so imperfect?
- If God has fulfilled all my needs, why am I still needy?
- If I'm forgiven, if Christ's shed blood washed away my sins and made me clean, why do I so often feel dirty and guilty?
- If I really am saved, why do I still do things I know are wrong?
- If God answers prayers, why isn't he answering mine?
- If Jesus has set me free, why am I still bound by addictions?

Some might question whether such individuals are really "saved." I was once told that because I still had doubts and questions about God and did not know the exact date of my "new birth," and because I had suffered with depression, I was not a true believer. Those same people told me that I would not be fully spiritual until I received a "heavenly language."

These well-meaning people spoke as though my childhood faith, my adolescent confirmation, and my lifetime of desiring to serve God meant nothing. For a short time I believed them and felt devastated. But eventually I came to see that they were wrong. While I believe in spiritual gifts, whether or not I received certain ones did not make me more or less spiritual.

In their desire to bring all people to Christ, they had adopted a set of rules for believers to follow—a mold into which they must fit—and labeled it "Christian." It isn't that easy.

God had begun to work in me from the moment I was conceived, perhaps even before (Ps. 139). I had chosen to believe at an early age. My struggles, doubts, and confusion were merely growing pains, the kind we all face as we move toward Christian maturity. I was right to be concerned and to ask questions. Curiosity and a willingness to pursue answers make us more aware of human shortcomings and imperfections. Questioning opens the door to self-examination and draws us continuously closer to God (2 Cor. 13:5). We must be careful about being too quick to offer formulas or legalistic jargon where God is concerned. Jesus himself said:

> "Not everyone who says to Me, 'Lord, Lord,' shall enter the kingdom of heaven, but he who does the will of My Father in heaven. Many will say to me in that day, 'Lord, Lord, have we not prophesied in Your name, cast out demons in Your name, and done many wonders in Your name?'
>
> And then I will declare to them, 'I never knew you; depart from Me, you who practice lawlessness.'"
>
> Matthew 7:21–23 NKJV

Perhaps we'd do better asking ourselves "Am I doing God's will?" and "Am I growing more Christlike?" rather than asking whether we are following the "right" set of rules. We are not all alike, nor do we all have the same spiritual experiences. We are unique, and God reveals himself according to our individual needs and ability to understand.

As you come to God and open yourself up to the Holy Spirit's work in your life, try not to be discouraged by people who think they have all the answers or who try to fit you into a certain mold they label as "Christian." These molds, while they may contain many truths, far too often limit God's power and presence within us.

In *A Circle of Quiet,* Madeleine L'Engle says, "When I get dogmatic about such weighty matters it is usually when I am most unsure of myself."[1] I think that's true for many of us. Whenever I hear an opinionated person insisting that we must live this way or that, I wonder if he or she, too, might not be outwardly bold but inwardly quivering with uncertainty.

We dare not attempt to confine God to our formulated guidelines or, like the Pharisees Christ chastened (Matt. 23), we may block the work and true healing God wants to do in our lives.

The "Healer"

Once I went to hear an evangelist who advertised himself as a "healer." I watched as he called people with all kinds of medical and emotional problems up on stage to be healed.

People came. He recited Scripture passages about healing and faith and promised that if they had enough faith— if they truly believed and trusted in God—and if they were free of sin, they would be healed. Perhaps some of them were healed; I couldn't tell. But I remember two people who weren't: a little boy with muscular dystrophy, whose condition didn't change, and a man with cancer, who died a few weeks later.

The "healer" made it very clear that the problem was that either they still had sin in their lives or they didn't have enough faith. I questioned his opinion. Being healed inside and out is not as simple as having enough faith or trusting God enough. And if God only answered the prayers of those who had no sin, none of our prayers would ever be answered.

I hoped the "healer's" pronouncement that these hurting people were not good enough to be healed didn't turn them away from God. For, as we saw in Mark 19:17–24, faith for healing does not rest on the one who is sick, but on the healer.

I do not intend to judge or condemn this man or any of those who try to teach us God's way, but Christ does warn us to be wary of false teachers (2 Peter 2). All of us, because we lack complete understanding of God, can easily offer answers that are not necessarily from God. Nor am I suggesting I have answers others don't. What I am saying is that as much as we are able, we need to remain open to what God wishes to do in our lives and in the lives of others. We need to be wary of those who offer easy answers, as well as those who make holy living an impossible goal.

When the Church Hinders Healing

When Jesus died and rose again, he threw open the doors of the Garden. We can walk into it any time we want to. Unfortunately, few actually do it. Why? Perhaps because no one tells us we can.

Often, the first advice offered to new Christians is "Find a church." This is good advice since Paul tells us in Hebrews 10:25 that we should continue to meet together and encourage one another toward Christian maturity and wholeness. We are called to be a functioning part of the body of Christ (Rom. 12; 1 Cor. 12). We'll do well to find a healthy church in which we can enjoy our freedom in Christ and grow in faith.

Unfortunately, some religious organizations within the body of Christ do more to hinder spiritual growth than to promote it. All too often, instead of entering God's presence in the Garden, new believers walk through the doors of a church building, thinking they are headed toward freedom and a new life in Christ, when instead they may find themselves solidly ensconced in another shell.

Let me explain: The church, as the body of Christ, is a vital aspect of spiritual life as long as it is healthy, growing, dynamic, and productive. As David Johnson and Jeff VanVonderen say in their book, *The Subtle Power of Spiritual Abuse:*

Churches are meant to be safe places where spiritual leaders help and equip the members for the work of service. There are some churches, however, where leaders use their spiritual authority to control and dominate others, attempting to meet their own needs for importance, power, intimacy or spiritual gratification. Through the subtle use of the right "spiritual" words, church members are manipulated or shamed into certain behaviors and performances that ensnares in legalism, guilt and begrudging service.[2]

The church can be a vehicle that provides support and encouragement to those who wish to become whole and healed persons. It can be a place where broken people can come and feel welcome. It can offer educational opportunities and empower each person to fulfill his or her purpose in life. Sadly, many churches fail to serve this purpose, but instead act as self-perpetuating organisms that focus more on their political and social existence than on their Christ-commissioned mission.[3] Too often the church bears the image of a broken people rather than reflecting the image of God. Let me offer a few examples.

"I first became a believer at a Billy Graham crusade about twenty years ago," Emily told me. "I prayed that God would come into my life and heal me. I was thrilled with the knowledge that I had been saved and that from that point on, life would be different. It was. And it wasn't."

When I asked what she meant, Emily said, "I was immediately 'plugged into a church.' Within a few months I became disillusioned and frustrated. I saw so much hypocrisy. It seemed that the pastor preached more on tithing and building a new church than on God."

Another friend recently left her church after twenty years. "The church is stagnant," she explained. "It should be pregnant with new life and new hope. I've tried to make a difference, but I feel like I'm fighting an incoming tide. I guess, in all fairness, I shouldn't be so critical. They are all good people. I think they are just so afraid of moving in the wrong direction that they won't move at all."

All too often, caring, concerned people who mean only to show us their view of God and humanity actually end up trying to corral us into stained-glass prisons, while God's Holy Spirit yearns to set us free.[4] This, it seems to me, is one of the more serious symptoms of the Humpty Dumpty Syndrome. We are so used to living within the confines of our shells that we don't fully understand the concept of freedom. Consequently, we adopt narrow-minded, worldly views of God and ourselves rather than the liberating, dynamic views that more accurately reflect restored humanity and the omniscience of God.

The accompanying diagram illustrates my point. In figure 1, we see the believer moving out of an expansive world into the narrow way (through Christ) and coming into the church. The church here is smaller than the world, restricted and boxed in, with only a narrow opening. This first model shows the church as a prison of sorts, where one learns the rules and conforms to the mold. It is by its very nature confining and uncomfortable.

Figure 1. The Confining, or worldly, view.

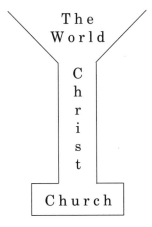

For those who experience church like this, life is often oppressive. The light in which we are supposed to walk is filtered through stained-glass windows, or through the small opening where we once met Christ. We hover near the light, trying to be content. We tell ourselves this is the moral and right way to live and that we must persevere. We repeat our testimonies to remind us that we have indeed been saved and long for the future, when Christ will come again to set us free. We rely on pastors or priests to guide us closer to the light, only to find that they too are walking in darkness.

From our stained-glass prisons we repeatedly call out to others to join us and wonder why they don't jump at the chance. If your church feels like a human fortress, you may want to ask yourself, "Is this really what God had in mind for us when he sent Christ into the world to redeem and restore us?" I don't think so.

God's Plan to Restore Us

God's plan for restoration has basically two parts, *justification* and *sanctification.*

Justification makes us right with God and brings us to the place where we can be reformed and transformed. According to theologian Thomas Langford, "Sanctification is built upon justification and constitutes the goal, or true end, of human life. Justification opens the way to a new life; sanctification is the heart of religion and the goal of Christian living."[5]

In justification God tears down the wall that sin built around the Garden. He opens his arms and gives us the opportunity to start again. Every person, regardless of gender, age, race, or position, has direct access to God. We are free to enter the holy of holies, to be with God whenever we please. God waits, hoping we will come closer.

A friend and I were discussing how few people seem to know about this freedom. "Most people," Jim said, "treat religion as if it were a jail sentence. They get caught up in the straight and narrow path and never make it to the kingdom. Actually, when Christ talked about the narrow way, I think he was referring to the entry, rather than to the inner sanctuary."

I could relate well to his concept. For a long time I tended to see Christianity and the "way" to healing and eternal life as this church-shaped place with stained glass windows—a sort of shrine where we learned how to act and what to say.

I was a Christian, but I didn't seem to be going anywhere. The promises of joy and an abundant life seemed like distant thunder rolling in the hills behind my imagination. I thought I was walking on the path, but it didn't seem right.

Caught along the Way

It takes more than just believing to be fully restored. Feeling convicted, turning to God, and accepting his gift of forgiveness are only the beginning. "Real religion," John Wesley tells us, is Christ restoring humanity to perfection, "not only to the favour but also to the Image of God."[6]

Real and complete healing, then, happens only when we are restored to the image of God and to a healthy, intimate relationship with him. This means we undergo a major transformation. Once we are healed, we will be different and new.

God used the most painful time in my life—my depression—to show me that even though I had chosen to follow Jesus, I hadn't gone far enough. I was like the people Jim talked about who thought that living the Christian life meant living in cramped quarters.

I'd come to a dead end in my life and God was there to pick up the pieces of my broken dreams. Without interference from me, God picked me up and pieced me together with Holy Glue. He reshaped and remolded me until I felt like a new person, restored and ready to face the world. His Holy Glue contained the perfect balance of love, acceptance, forgiveness, and the power to protect me from evil.

Enveloped in God's love and strength, I found comfort and peace, yet I sensed my journey to wholeness had only just begun.

As I looked back, I realized I had gotten caught in the church cycle. Instead of using it as a vehicle leading to God, I was stuck there, hung up on jargon, shoulds, and can'ts.

In my helpless and broken state I placed myself in God's hands. Jesus carried me beyond the church, the walls, and the gate, and presented me to God.

There I saw that the narrow path led from a small, world-shaped prison cell into God's dominion.

"You Shall Be Free Indeed"

I believe that when God sent his Son to die for us and to set us free, he had something entirely different in mind. For much of my adult life I saw Christianity as the confining environment of the first model. After all, Jesus said, "Enter by the narrow gate; for wide is the gate and broad is the way that leads to destruction, and there are many who go in by it. Because narrow is the gate and difficult is the way which leads to life, and there are few who find it" (Matt. 7:13–14 NKJV).

The gate is narrow. Jesus says getting through it is as difficult as threading a camel through a needle's eye (Matt. 19:24). Our inflated egos and our pride—that I-can-do-it-myself mentality—bloat us up and keep us from squeezing through. Once we accept our limitations, once we cry out to God to forgive us and to help us through, once we believe (even though we may have doubts), God guides us through the gate into his presence. His presence is not confined to buildings, but fills the heavens and the earth. He does not reside in a single, finite space but in infinity. Therefore, though we as humans are limited by natural and physical laws, when we allow God's Spirit to enter and fill us, our souls are set free and we become, in a sense limitless—infinite—and we gain eternity.

Figure 2 shows the world, not the church, as a prison. Beyond the world we see a portal, then freedom. The church here includes all the saints (all of us who have entered and who have become part of the body of Christ), with no denominational walls or barriers. Reconciled to God, we enter into the process of being re-created in God's image—of being made holy.

Figure 2. The liberating, dynamic view.

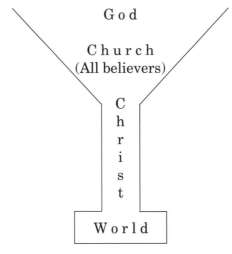

As we enter the church, we enter a wide, wonder-filled world. It is an eternally timeless, spiritual panorama which, like God, has no beginning and no end. The church is like the Garden God originally created for his children.

Here we are free to roam, free to explore, and free to grow. Here the older, more mature saints encourage, empower, and enlighten the young and help them experience the fullness of God.

In this nurturing place, we are free to become the men and women God created us to be. We are not bound by laws, but are encouraged to develop moral integrity. We still have boundaries, but they are determined by love, not by law (Rom. 6:14). Jesus established the boundaries of the Garden by saying:

> As the Father loved Me, I also have loved you; abide in My love. If you keep My commandments, you will abide in My love, just as I have kept My Father's commandments and abide in His love.
>
> These things I have spoken to you, that My joy may remain in you, and that your joy may be full. This is My commandment, that you love one another as I have loved you.
>
> John 15:9–12 NKJV

When love determines our boundaries we don't need legalistic statutes to guide us. As Paul states in Romans 6:14, "You are not under law but under grace." And in Romans 13:10 (NKJV) he says that "Love does no harm to a neighbor; therefore love is the fulfillment of the law."

We have the freedom to make our own choices, but our choices have consequences. Like Adam and Eve, certain things we do can harm us and cause us to fall again. Consequently, we will want to be careful to filter our choices through the light of Christ's love by asking these questions: Am I acting out of love? Am I doing what Christ would do?

A church set in the Garden will never build walls that restrict those who do not conform but will always reach out to build bridges so that all may know Christ's love and enter into relationship with him.

"But, how do we deal with those who willfully disobey God?" you may be asking. Sadly, there will be those who turn away, or who deliberately choose to walk in the darkness rather than in the light. Like Jesus, we'll want to have compassion, remember them in prayer, avoid judgmental attitudes, and in true humility, as one who has also been broken, offer them a hand when their world comes crashing down around them.

Scripture gives us guidelines for living with people who walk in darkness. Romans 12:17–21 (NKJV) tells us:

> Repay no one evil for evil. Have regard for good things in the sight of all men. If it is possible, as much as depends on you, live peaceably with all men. Beloved, do not avenge yourselves, but rather give place to wrath; for it is written, "Vengeance is Mine, I will repay," says the Lord. . . . Do not be overcome by evil, but overcome evil with good.

The Bible also tells us we are to confront those within the body who do wrong in a spirit of gentleness, remembering that we could just as easily have fallen (Gal. 6:1).

Outside the Garden

As I mentioned earlier, the church can be one of the greatest hindrances to wholeness. While some Christian leaders want to lead people to Christ, they all too often send them away again by trying to mold them and God into their own distorted views of God and the church. They are, in a sense, standing at the Garden gate saying, "If you want to enter, you must be like us and obey our rules." They forget that coming to the Garden and living a holy life are not the same as going to a social organization and plugging into various activities. It is, rather, coming to know and love God and growing in one's faith.

Sadly, the church today, the body of Christ, is broken, and in need of repair and restoration. The church is only as healed and holy as the people who comprise it. As God's people reflect his image, so does the church. And that image can be changed only as we become whole.

Even though many of our churches are unhealthy, many, too, are dynamic, alive, and glorifying God. And we have many strong spiritual leaders who have found healing and who do reflect God's image. These leaders strive to help the body of Christ function as a whole unit. I encourage you to find those who offer support, encouragement, and provide an environment that stimulates emotional and spiritual growth.

Coming to the Garden

Perhaps you recognize your need for God and for restoration and for forgiveness of sins, yet because you're not used to being restored, you continue to live broken. In a sense you may feel like Kent, a burn victim. Bandages covered his entire face. Hours after the accident, Kent awoke and opened his eyes. "I'm blind!" he cried.

"No," the nurse reassured him. "You're not blind. You just can't see through the bandages. When we remove them you'll be able to see just fine."

We are not wearing bandages, but we do often enter the Garden fully covered by the shells we've so carefully constructed in order to protect our vulnerable inner selves. In order to see the Garden and experience all God has for us, we must remove them.

This is not easy. Our shells are the only identity some of us have. So we are faced with a dilemma: Do we continue to wear our shells and limit God in our lives, or do we break out of our self-imposed prisons?

I suspect that if you could, you'd escape. But how? You can begin by loosening your hold on what you perceive reality to be. You can say, "I will release my old beliefs and attitudes and ask God to replace them with his truth. I want to poke holes in my shell so that the pure, cleansing breath of God can enter me and give me life."

We may not be able to step away from the shell completely or all at once. That would take a great deal of trust and faith in what we can't see or understand. Perhaps we can, however, break out a small window that will allow us to gain closer access to God and to the image of God in ourselves and in others.

In the next chapter we'll focus on breaking out of our shells so we can more fully enjoy the freedom Jesus has given us. Before we do, however, take out your journal and reflect on your view of Christianity and the church.

1. Look at the two diagrams again. Which better describes your idea of the church and sainthood?
2. Which better describes your present church?
3. Do you know anyone who is imprisoned by legalistic thinking? (Legalistic thinkers imply that you are not really a Christian if you break their spoken and unspoken religious rules.)
4. Imagine yourself walking from a dark world, permeated by evil. As you exit this prison, you enter a narrow space—a tunnel. You see a light shining at the other end. You walk forward. On the way you meet Jesus. You see his birth and his life, and you experience his unconditional love. You witness his death, and you stand at the foot of the cross and weep.

    Then you accompany the women to the tomb on the third day, but Jesus is gone. An angel at the tomb tells you Jesus has risen. Elated, you run to tell the others, but they don't believe you. Then Jesus appears and all doubts are gone as you touch his nail-scarred hands and feet. He shows you where the sword pierced his side and you know: Jesus *is* alive.

He takes your hand and walks you to the gate. He opens it and escorts you into the Garden.

Jesus tells you that you do not enter alone. He sends along a part of himself—the comforter, the Holy Spirit—to walk with you.

Close your eyes and let yourself see and feel this encounter with Jesus with your inner eye, your heart, your spirit, and your soul. After you have done this, write your impressions.

Coming into the Garden can be a wondrous, breath-taking experience. It can also be frightening, like stepping forward to meet royalty when you are dressed in filthy rags.

8

A Prisoner
of Fear

"I DON'T UNDERSTAND IT." Sheila scrubbed at the tears spilling down her cheeks. "I believe in God, and I believe that Jesus died for me. I've been a Christian for years, but . . ."

"But . . ." I echoed, encouraging her to continue.

"I don't know. When I first became a Christian I was so happy, and I thought . . . anyway, I'd gotten the impression that things were supposed to get better. If anything, I feel worse than ever. I guess I'm just not a very good person."

"Do you really believe that?" I asked.

"I don't know what to believe. I read so many stories about people who give their lives to the Lord. I mean . . . I guess it reminds me of a fairy tale. Like Jesus is this prince on a white horse who slays the evil dragon, then rescues the princess and carries her to a secluded and beautiful castle on a hill where they live happily ever after. I felt kind of like that at first. Oh, I know the gospel isn't a fairy tale, but even the Bible says we're to live like king's kids and the brides of Christ."

She buried her face in her hands and wept. After a few moments she raised her head. "I don't feel like a princess. I just feel miserable. If God really has saved me, why do I feel so wretched? Didn't Jesus say he came to give us an abundant life? All I have an abundance of is trouble."

Sheila had accepted God's gift. She's right, according to John 10:10, Jesus did say, "I have come that they may have life, and that they may have it more abundantly" (NKJV). So what's wrong? Where is the joy, the peace, the happiness we're supposed to have as God's children? We are the king's kids, brides of the Prince of Peace, yet we often feel like paupers.

Despite her feelings, Sheila is still a believer. Like Michael, whose leg was amputated, she is having phantom pains. And like Keith, who thought he was blind, she can't see through her shell. She is also suffering from a condition that affects numerous believers today. She's forgotten to walk away from the old Sheila and embrace the new.

Far too many of us live like Cinderella, the poor, mistreated waif who was allowed to go to the ball. She finds the prince and falls in love. She tastes the joy of the dance. He embraces her and tells her of his love. Cindy delights in the heady sensations of new life, momentarily forgetting her status as a peasant girl. Suddenly the awareness strikes: "I'm not a princess. I've got to run before he discovers who I really am." At midnight she retreats and darkness swallows her. The dance is over and she's back in rags, hiding in the ashes and wondering if it ever really happened.

When the Dance Is Over

Like Cinderella, we hide, too, not in ashes and rags, but behind the patched-up shells we've built around ourselves to guard against hurt and abuse. If we would dare to step away from those shells, we would discover that we have been transformed. Our souls are no longer dirty and broken but made new and beautiful by the transforming power of the divine Prince. If we would discard our shells and come out of hiding, we'd see that God's love—his Holy Glue—is all the protection we'll ever need.

The tragedy is that far too many of us never see the transformation of our souls because we remain trapped in those faulty, crusted shells.

Cinderella fled so no one could see what she really was. She felt ashamed, fearful, and full of pride. In her defense, however, I have to say, the shell may have been the only face she really knew, and she may have feared she wouldn't survive if she lost it.

Deep inside we know that holding on to our shells keeps us from living the kind of life God wants for us, and if we are ever to feel free, fully healed, and whole, the shell must eventually be discarded.

Knowing something must be done and doing it are two different things. We hang back because of our fears. We often pass up the chance to be healed because we're afraid of the changes being well and whole might bring. That may sound strange, but it's true.

Maggie lived in a deplorable situation. Her husband went into drunken rages and beat her regularly for years. She finally gathered enough courage to leave him. Why had she stayed so long? "My life with Hal was awful, but at least I knew what to expect," she told me. "I was so afraid of what would happen to me and the kids if I left him. It was my fear, not Hal's beatings, that kept me a prisoner."

Just as Maggie was a prisoner of her fear, so too are those who hide behind their shells. Fear of the unknown keeps us from being all that we were meant to be. When our vulnerable self becomes threatened, we make excuses. Our defense mechanisms jump into action. We begin asking questions like these:

- Why expose myself to the pain de-shelling myself would bring? Is this really necessary?
- Can't I just be happy and accept me the way I am, cracks, glue, patches, and all?
- Isn't God's grace and love—that Holy Glue—sufficient?

In part, yes. In him we do find answers and the strength and peace to cope with life's problems. And yes, if we choose to stay safely tucked inside our shells, he will still hold us. God loves us regardless of the condition we're in—shell or no shell, broken or healed. Perhaps we can even find some semblance of happiness there. But is that what God really wants for us? Is that what we want for ourselves?

"Can we ever fully discard our shells?" my friend Carla asked. "Basically, it comes down to trust, doesn't it? I'm not sure I'll ever have absolute trust—even in God—so I don't know if I can ever let the shell go completely."

"We do need trust . . . and courage. Neither comes easily for me," I replied. "Certainly we'll never trust perfectly, but I think we can trust enough. And what we lack, God will supply. Initially, what's important isn't so much that we let go of our shells all at once, but that we are honest about their existence. Maybe even more than trust and courage, we need the desire to be free and a willingness to let God help us."

Stepping Out

You'll recall that for a time after the dance, Cinderella stayed in the ashes, only dreaming of her life with the prince. If she had continued to hide, he may never have found her. In a great act of courage, she stepped forward and spoke to the prince. She made herself vulnerable. Her honesty and humility brought her face to face with one who had the power to transform her. She slipped her foot into the glass slipper he offered, became a new person, and rode with him into another, far superior world.

When Christ reconciles us to himself, we are transformed. At conception, an egg is transformed as it is fertilized and re-created into a new life—a new creature. The fertilized egg gives way to a viable new life because it has been permeated by another presence and changed. The egg doesn't reach its full potential unless it is inseminated and allowed to become the free creature it was intended to be.

We, too, can become new creatures with vast potential once we have been made viable by the presence of God's Holy Spirit in our lives. God permeates the membranes of our souls. He plants a seed—a part of his being, the Holy Spirit—in us and we become new creatures.

For as much time as we need, God then broods over us. He waits until we are ready, and then, at the appointed time, our shells fall away and we emerge ready to face the world. Far too often we refuse to discard our old shells. We imprison our souls and keep ourselves from being all that God wants us to be.

Paula's Vision

Paula, a friend and soul mate, and I were discussing the topic of my book one day when she said, "I lived inside a shell for many years. I always felt inadequate, insecure. I had this longing inside me to be more than what I had become. But I thought I was just being selfish, so I ignored it and kept trying to complete myself through my family and doing things for others. I'd always been taught that you shouldn't think about your own needs and that you should always be serving others."

"What happened to change that?" I asked.

"It was weird," she said as she paused to take a sip of her tea. "One day I was in the kitchen doing dishes and I noticed a little bird outside my window. It's hard to explain, but part of me suddenly felt trapped. I wanted to be out there, flying.

"I get goose bumps just thinking about it, because in that moment God showed me that he wanted me to fly, too. I know it sounds strange, but I felt like he was saying, 'Paula, you have my Spirit in you. I have made you a new creature and have great plans for you, but you keep yourself locked up. Let go.'"

"And did you?" I asked.

"Not at first. I was scared. I didn't know what to do. I prayed. I told God I was willing to do anything if he'd help me. It's funny, you know. I expected to get this sudden flash of insight, but nothing happened. After a couple of days, I forgot about the vision, but a few months later I was reading a book called *Outgrowing the Pain* by Elaina Gil. I'm not sure why, but I'd seen it in the bookstore and felt like I really needed to read it."

"Were you abused as a child?" I asked.

"Not physically, but my mom was a perfectionist and I never felt like I could measure up. Anyway, when Gil talked about how we protect ourselves and build walls, I realized I'd locked away a vital part of myself. I knew that if I were to discover my full potential as a human being and a Christian I'd have to escape from my shell. I wanted to, but for the longest time, I didn't know how."

A Plan of Escape

The Bible tells us that part of God's plan for us is to "work out our own salvation" (Phil. 2:12). Perhaps this giving up our shells and abandoning ourselves to the way God wants us to live is, at least in part, what that directive means. God wants to save us from our prisons and give us new life, but we, in a real sense, hold the keys to our own cells. We must decide whether or not we want to escape and if, once we are free, we can handle that freedom.

Escaping our shells requires a great deal of work. Not only do we need to make a break for it, we need to adjust to our new lifestyle and make changes in the way we act and think that reflect the new person we've become. We need to shed the prison mentality and live in the light of freedom. And finally, we need to take certain steps to avoid being imprisoned again.

When we move from the darkness of the world into the brilliance of God's garden, we cannot help but see our flaws. God calls us to come to him, yet we often hold back. A part of us, the new creature growing within, is anxious to go, but another part, the shell self, holds back. We are like a woman torn between two loves, being faithful to neither. Fear of the unknown, shame for the past, and perhaps even commitment to remain intact keep us bound to the shell lifestyle. We are, in a sense, married to the shell. It has become one with us, and without it we may feel incomplete, confused, and insecure.

As prisoners of our patched-up shells, we have several options. We can stay inside and never fully experience what it means to be reconciled to self, God, and others. We can make a peephole and be content with only a glimpse of what life is like on the outside. We can live a hermit-crab existence—step out of the shell now and then, but drag it behind us so we can pop into it when we feel threatened.

Before we choose those options, however, we may want to consider what happens to eggs that never hatch: They rot. Unless we accept the new life God has given us, step free of our shells, and let the Spirit of God breathe life into us, we will become stagnant, dull, and dry. Unless we break free, we'll suffocate the new life growing in us.

Another option, one I highly recommend, is to cast our fears to the wind and loosen our grip on face-saving pride. We can trust that God will hold us, and make a break for it.

How do we do that? I promised early on that this book would not be filled with easy answers. It does not tell you the problem and then say, "Get your act together." Rather, it embraces the problems and looks into our fears and the struggles we have when making changes, even when we know the changes are right.

In the next chapter, we'll hear from some people who have broken out and discover some ways in which we can gain the courage to let go of our shells and come fully into God's presence without shame, and say, "Hi, God. I'm home!"

9

Breaking
Out

DAN HAD BEEN RAISED by a controlling, overbearing father. "A large portion of my shell," Dan said, "was made up of bitterness and hatred toward my father. I found that was the hardest part of the shell to step away from. The shell was like a shield that I could hold up to show people I'd been a victim. If I held the shield, I had an excuse for acting out, for failure.

"When you discard that part of your shell, you put the past behind you and say, 'Yes, I was abused, but I'm not going to use that as an excuse anymore. Yes, it hurt and left scars, but if I'm to grow into the person I want to be—that God wants me to be—I need to give it up.' It was hard, but I finally handed my patch of hatred and bitterness to God.

"It's funny," Dan added. "I've been in counseling for years. I thought hashing and rehashing the story in therapy was helping me. But every time I told someone, I'd grow more angry. I finally realized I was just causing more pain by reliving the experiences. I think what has helped me the most is having this visual picture of myself breaking out. I see myself crashing through the walls of anger, bitterness, resentment, fear, shame, and a hundred other things that hold me in. In God I have someone who loves and protects me and teaches me what being human is all about. And somehow that's enough. Since I've been able to take an objective view, I see that my dad was caught in his own brokenness. He didn't know how to love because no one ever showed him. I don't hate him anymore. I feel sorry for him and hope someday he can escape his prison as well."

Dan has managed to discard his shell. He came to see that the shell wasn't really a part of himself, but a shield he carried to protect his vulnerable broken self.

A Shell of Protection

In my journey to wholeness, the hardest move I had to make was to walk away from the shell and come face to face with God. My shell had served as a cover-up and a shield that kept me from taking chances or doing anything that might embarrass me or take me out of my safety zone.

When I fell apart in depression, I also saw that God's love had woven a cocoon of Holy Glue around me. In it I felt safe and protected. I accepted God's gift of eternal life and knew God loved me. I danced with my prince but, like Sheila, after a time I felt the dance had ended. I hurried back into my shell full of fear, pride, guilt, and shame. I still lacked trust. I felt insecure and didn't want anyone, not even God, to get too close. Intimacy meant exposing myself—I wasn't ready for that.

Yet something about me had changed. In my depressed state, my cover was blown. I began to realize that people loved me no less when they saw how weak, vulnerable, and imperfect I was. As I began to share my experiences, I noticed that when I was real with people, they loved me even more. Well, maybe not everyone. Some were offended by my honesty and would have preferred the shell.

I often sensed that inner voice I'd come to recognize as God's saying, *"You don't need that shell. Trust me. Let go. I have so much more to offer."* I wanted to trust God, wanted to believe in and accept the life God offered, but I was afraid.

The Battle for Freedom

The Holy Glue was transparent, so I couldn't always be sure it was there. If I discarded my old shell, patched and dilapidated as it was, I would expose the fragile, vulnerable part of me—or at least that's what I told myself. I discovered later that what I really feared was that this new creature growing inside of me—the one God had restored—would recklessly respond to God and abandon common sense. Sometimes that new part of me cried out like a wounded child wanting to be heard and seen, but my old self, like a controlling parent, refused to listen.

Occasionally, the new me won despite my protestations—like the time she told God that she would do anything he wanted her to do, then signed up for the Evangelism Explosion program at church. Nothing the shell could say seemed to deter her. She was developing an intimate relationship with God. I think that scared me most of all.

She loved him far too much and would do anything he asked just to please him. She was uninhibited, impetuous, and impulsive, and she adored God. She even envisioned herself standing in front of hundreds of people sharing her testimony and sharing God's love with people. You can understand why I needed the shell to keep a tight reign on her.

As I think about how I tried to inhibit my restored self, I'm reminded of a story about King David in 2 Samuel 6:14–22: David had just brought the ark of the covenant to Jerusalem. He was so full of joy he "danced before the

Lord with all his might." His wife, Michal, saw him in the courtyard wearing nothing but an apron. He was out there in front of God and everybody "leaping and whirling." Michal was angry and embarrassed, and "despised him in her heart."

When he came in, she said, "How glorious was the king of Israel today, uncovering himself in the eyes of the maids of his servants, as one of the base fellows shamelessly uncovers himself!"

"It was before the Lord," David responded, "and I will be even more undignified than this. I will be humble in my own sight."

My insecure self could relate to Michal. I felt that way toward my new self when she abandoned protocol. She probably would have danced naked and unashamed before the Lord too, had I not made certain she was covered. Fortunately, the Michal in me had her weak moments, or the new creature I'd become may have been destroyed.

One time I gave in to her desire to play with clay and ended up becoming a production potter. I have to admit, she was right about that one—even the inhibited me loved the feel of clay squishing through my hands, of being a creator again. She brought back a part of me I'd lost in the fall—the artist.

Later she insisted that I become a writer. Lord knows I didn't want to subject myself to the rejection that kind of life might bring. But the new me loved it and knew it was what God wanted. The old me resisted, of course. "You can't possibly make it," I'd argue. "You're not an expert. You don't have what it takes."

I managed to come up with enough excuses to hold her back for a while, but her faith in God and her self-esteem grew stronger every day.

In the end, I went along reluctantly, knowing that stepping into the unknown would probably result in more fractures that would have to be repaired. I was right. My first book, *Have You Hugged Your Teenager Today,* brought invitations to appear on radio and TV talk shows. I was asked to speak to large groups, and my new self accepted. I didn't panic, at least not right away. I simply reminded her that she was not a princess and that she had no business acting like one.

I'd spent a lifetime reconstructing and remodeling my shell. The new creature inside me threatened to cut loose and throw it off. Afraid to take chances, afraid of failure, afraid of success, afraid that God might ask the impossible, I stood firm—well, as firm as I could against the uninhibited new me. My shell, once a protective shield for a wounded spirit, had become a prison to my restored soul.

Fortunately, my new self did not comply. God has shown me how to love and nurture the fearful part of me, to re-parent the child in me who needed shells to feel safe. The Spirit-filled, new creature is winning. As my faith and trust in God grows, the shell is falling away, piece by piece, and I'm learning to love the new creature I'm becoming.

Are You Holding On?

Dan and I have given our views about shells, and now I'd like you to take a few moments to look at yours.

1. Do you hide inside a shell? If so, take some time to evaluate it.
2. How did it began to take shape and what is it like now?
3. Does it serve a purpose?
4. Do you still need it? Sometimes a shell is like a security blanket that we won't give up until it's worn down to a piece of lint—and then we replace it.

Once you've expressed your feelings about your old shell and its effectiveness, you're ready for the next step—releasing the person inside.

Releasing the Person Inside

Remember Paula from the last chapter? As you'll recall, Paula's shell had developed early on when she was forced to protect her vulnerable self as a small child. "As a child," she said, "I loved to color, draw, and paint. Watercolor and finger painting were my favorites. My mother would frown with irritation every time I wanted to paint. In her rush to tidy up and keep the house neat, she gave me the message that painting was not an acceptable behavior."

Paula's creativity was stifled, and she simply stopped being an artist. She stopped being spontaneous, being honest, being transparent, and being innocent. Eventually she formed the habit of *doing* and forgot how to *be* Paula.

"My mother abused me," Paula said, "but I realize now that I have abused myself, too, by neglecting my spirit and not meeting the needs of my inner self. I'm having to learn how to nurture and love the new me."

"And you're painting again," I suggested.

Paula nodded. "Yes. In fact, one of the first things I did was to go out and buy a sheet of plasterboard and a set of finger paints. I dressed in a worn T-shirt and jeans, got down on my hands and knees, and stayed there until I'd covered every inch of the plasterboard. I had paint on every part of my body. When it was done, I leaned back on my haunches and looked at it. Then it hit me. I remembered the little bird on my windowsill and I knew. I didn't just happen to have this urge to paint. Somehow I'd broken through the shell and God was teaching me how to fly."

Not everyone rescues the new creature inside by playing in clay or finger painting. These methods are simply analogous of the real principle behind them—that of freeing the new creature growing inside of us. By playing—whether it's finding cloud creatures in the sky, flying a kite, dancing in a sunlit meadow, or running on the beach—we regain the sense of wonder, imagination, intuitiveness, and freedom to believe in miracles.

In a sense, we are given a new chance to grow up again. No matter how terrible our old life, we have the hope of a new life in Christ.

Shells keep us from reaching our full potential. Once we take the shell away, we find a new creature who, like a child, needs to be nurtured and held—re-parented in a way that will promote happiness and a full, rich abundant life.

I hope, like Sheila, Paula, Dan, and I, you have chosen to discard your shell and come out of hiding. God really does have an abundant life waiting for you that is far beyond your imagination.

When I came forward, I came trembling. The Lord embraced me. I felt God's power and strength and knew that I could leave my shell behind. God lifted me and carried me into a new world. Please don't get me wrong. I'm not suggesting that life with God and without the shell takes place in a sterile environment where everything is perfect and wonderful and painless. There is no happy-ever-after land, except of course, in heaven.

Yet our home with God is a place where we don't have to be afraid to feel and to be ourselves. We don't need our shells because God's love protects us. It's a place where we are free to explore, expand our interests, spread our wings, and develop into mature persons. And it's a place where, even when the world is falling down around us, our souls can find harmony and contentment. Though we experience loss and pain, we have hope as God's love surrounds and permeates us and our circumstances. A few years ago I wrote a poem expressing this kind of holy hopefulness, which first appeared in my book *What Kids Need Most in a Mom*:

> God gives me hope in hopeless situations,
> And helps me see the rainbow
> On the other side of rain.

He heals the thorn-infested wounds
That I might delight in roses.
He gives me tears to wash away the pain;
Oh, but then . . . then . . .
He gives me joy so I can laugh again.

Hope helps me cope and helps me to walk shell-free into each tomorrow. I pray it can do the same for you.

Have you stepped out of your shell? If so, that's great. If you're still wrapped inside it, that's okay too. Letting go takes a great deal of faith and trust in God and confidence in one's new self, and that takes time. Perhaps these will come as we move into the final chapters and learn how to care for the new self.

10

Adjusting
to the New You

Most human beings today waste twenty-five to
thirty years of their lives before they break
through the actual and conventional lies which
surround them.

Isadora Duncan

I'D WASTED ABOUT THIRTY-TWO YEARS. How about you? Once I decided to step away from my shell, I realized why so few people ever come this far in the healing process. The work can at times be tedious and exhausting. I understood what British essayist and novelist G. K. Chesterton (1874–1936) meant when he wrote, "The Christian ideal has not been tried and found wanting. It has been found difficult and left untried."[1]

As we move from life in the shell to whatever new adventures God has in store for us, we'll need to learn what being whole (holy) entails. When I came to the place where I decided to give up my shell, I felt anything but finished. So much had changed, inside and out. I wasn't the same

131

person I'd been. I was like a character in a witness-protection program with a new identity. I felt out of balance, unfocused, disoriented, and frightened. I'd been given a new life, but I wasn't sure what to do with it. One of the first things I needed to do was to finalize my separation from the shell, the old or false self, and come to terms with residual feelings.

Divorcing Your Shell

As anyone who has been divorced or who has left an unhealthy relationship knows, your love for that person doesn't change simply because you walk away. It isn't easy to change a lifetime of patterns and beliefs. Because of our innate ability to maintain equilibrium and bring things back into balance, we may find ourselves slipping into old habits because they are more comfortable and easier to live with than the new.

Marla left her husband, David, because he'd been unfaithful to her several times during their ten-year marriage. "It was so hard not to go back to him," Marla said. "David didn't want the divorce. He told me he would change, and I almost believed him. He'd asked me to come over to his place and talk about it. I said no, but after a while I changed my mind and decided to go." Marla sighed and let out a shaky breath. "He was with another woman. Even after that I considered just closing my eyes and letting him have his affairs. I'd done it before. I thought maybe I could pretend it didn't hurt, pretend it wasn't happening. That's how scared I was of being alone."

"But you didn't go back," I said.

"No. I knew I couldn't live like that any more. Seeing them together like that . . . I knew I couldn't pretend it wasn't happening. I had to face the fact that we had a lousy relationship. I filed for divorce. The only problem is, I still love him. Divorce may be final on paper, but not in the heart."

Like Marla, we also need time to adjust—time to put our lives in order. Putting ourselves together again and staying whole requires that we care for and nurture our new selves. We do that by maintaining a healthy environment that promotes growth and instills godly or Christlike qualities in us. The first mainstay to a healthy environment for the new self is openness and honesty.

When we move from one life to another we naturally carry some emotional baggage with us. It's important that we are open and honest about these emotions. As new creatures, we may feel that we should suddenly be transformed. We may expect ourselves to behave as though the old life never existed. What foolishness.

Would you expect a new baby to start acting like an adult the moment he is born? Would you expect a new widow to immediately be happy the moment she leaves the grave site? Of course not. Likewise, we can't expect the new self to experience instant change.

In Christ we are healed and given new identities. The effect is immediate, but because we are so emotionally complex, it may take our minds time to catch up with what has happened in our souls. We've experienced some major losses. Perhaps the first item of our self-care agenda will be to take a little time to grieve.

Taking Time to Grieve

When a drastic change occurs in our lives, such as illness, death of a loved one, or divorce, we experience loss. Marla, in losing her husband, lost an important part of herself. She lost a partner, a marriage, a home, and a lifestyle. Even though her life with David had been unhealthy, the loss was still real and painful.

We experience our first loss at birth, when we are separated from the security of our mother's womb. This change is necessary if we are to become viable human beings, but it still causes discomfort until we are able to make the necessary adjustments to life on the outside.

We also experience loss when we ditch our shells and are reborn as new creatures in Christ. Even though our shells were poorly constructed and unhealthy, they provided a measure of security. And, even though we are better off without them, we can expect to grieve the loss of the old self.

Most mental health and medical professionals are aware of the importance of the grieving process in coping with losses, yet many people resist working through their grief, or at least want to hurry the process along. In both my personal and professional experience I've found that grief will have its place whether we want it to or not. If we suppress it, our tangled emotions will build into anger, rage, guilt, shame, or depression. If not properly managed, suppressed grief can cause severe mental, physical, and even spiritual damage.

We need time to consider our losses and to say good-bye. We need to give ourselves permission to miss what we once had. Grief is normal. Let it happen, understand it, accept it, and then, when your grief is spent, move on to the exciting, though difficult, responsibility of living a new life.

As we come to terms with grief, we also need to recognize our vulnerability. Whenever change occurs, there's usually a tension, an uncertainty. Brokenness, rebirth, and shell demolition certainly qualify as change.

Being Vulnerable

Opening ourselves up and being real allows healing to take place. It also makes us more vulnerable. The moment we step out of our shells, we face the possibility of another fall. We are like newly hatched sparrows, vulnerable and easy prey. One false move can topple the young birds out of the nest and land them bruised and broken on the earth below, where predators lie in wait. Entirely dependent, they trust their mother to care for them. Freedom from shells can be dangerous.

One of the things we often do when trying to cope with grief is to find ways to protect this vulnerable self. In *How to Say Goodbye,* grief counselors Joanne Smith and Judy Biggs discuss five unhealthy coping mechanisms people use in handling grief:

- Illness: ailments, symptoms, and sympathy
- Lethargy: checking out
- Promiscuity: fill my empty arms
- Busyness syndrome: run till you drop
- Worrying: fear running wild

When we discard one shell we often set right to work developing another, perhaps even thicker, shell. These unhealthy coping mechanisms provide the fabric and glue we need to protect the new creature we've become. Unhealthy coping mechanisms don't defuse our grief, anger, confusion, and whatever other emotional burdens we carry; instead, they entomb them within where they will eventually explode and leave us even more broken than we were before. They are not a cure, but an excuse for not facing the reality of our situations.

We can add yet another coping mechanism to our list: superspirituality, or taking on religious character. Many adopt a pious attitude to avoid dealing with loss and grief. Grief is a painful process, so we buffer the effects by giving ourselves a spiritual face-lift.

As a leader in my church's Stephen Ministry, I teach a class called "Feelings: Yours, Mine, and Ours." The material gives an example of a woman who put up a spiritual front.

> There was a Christian wife and mother whose husband had died. Both wife and husband had been very active in their congregation before his death. Immediately after his death, rather than allowing anyone to minister to her, she kept a stiff upper lip and even sought to minister to those who came to the funeral. She felt that breaking down and openly mourning her loss would show a lack of faith in God and his goodness. Almost immediately after the funeral, the woman again became very active in her congregation. No one ever saw her shed a tear; she always had a happy face. About six months after her husband's death, she suddenly became very depressed. She took her infant son, went into the family car in the garage and asphyxiated both herself and her child.[2]

This is an extreme example, but it underscores the fact that people who do not deal effectively with their feelings and emotions may eventually find those feelings erupting and sending them totally out of control.

I'm convinced that it was this "stuffing" of my feelings and a fear of being honest and real with people that sent me over the edge into a full-blown depression from which I needed professional help to escape.

How Are You Feeling?

Be as honest with yourself and others as possible. If you have been guilty of using unhealthy coping mechanisms to deal with the changes, turmoil, and tragedies in your life, take out your journal and make that confession to God. Then tell God how you're feeling. Be honest. Be real.

Being real isn't easy. Sometimes it makes you cry. It means opening your heart for God and others to examine. Whenever I think about being real, I'm reminded of a familiar illustration that never seems to lose its appeal. No one explains being real better than this passage from *The Vel-veteen Rabbit* by Margery Williams:

"What is REAL?" asked the rabbit. . . . "Does it mean having things that buzz inside you and a stick-out handle?"

"Real isn't how you are made," said the Skin Horse. "It's a thing that happens to you. When a child loves you for a long time, not just to play with, but REALLY loves you, then you become Real."

"Does it hurt?" asked the Rabbit.

"Sometimes," said Skin Horse, for he was always truthful. "When you are Real you don't mind being hurt."

"Does it happen all at once, like being wound up," Rabbit asked, "or bit by bit?"

"It doesn't happen all at once," said the Skin Horse. "You become. It takes a long time. That's why it doesn't happen to people who break easily, or have sharp edges, or have to be carefully kept. Generally, by the time you are Real, most of your hair has been loved off, and your eyes drop out and you get loose in the joints and very shabby. But all these things don't matter at all, because once you are Real you can't be ugly, except to people who don't understand."[3]

An Enemy Lurks

We can be our own worst enemies when we choose to suppress our feelings. Yet another enemy lies in wait. When we have been set free and have decided to step away from our shells, we can bet that Satan, the king of bondage, is standing ready to try to capture us again. Evil hovers around us, waiting for an opportunity to house us in another shell. It waits for a time when we feel weak and think God is far away. As usual, evil wears a mask of social acceptance and goodwill. When it sees a need in us, it springs into action and offers assistance. The moment we weaken and begin to believe the lies, we're headed for another fall.

Because we need approval and are concerned about how we might look to others, Satan seeks to construct new shells out of imitation holiness. They will be built out of layers of false piety and lies that say we should act this way or that. We can get so caught up in playing the role of a good Christian—and become so involved in doing Christian work—that we lose sight of our real purpose.

When trouble comes and we feel God has deserted us, evil offers us protection, saying, "God doesn't care." In our confusion we may ask, "Why did God allow this or that?" Evil spreads rumors that whisper, "God is responsible for the world's toxic state."

The truth is, trouble exists because evil and humanity conspire against God. God, on the other hand, consistently provides us with a safety net. When we call on him to help us, he is there. When we ask forgiveness for falling into sin, God forgives. He covers us with mercy, love, and saving grace. God sent Christ to save and purify us, and the Holy Spirit to comfort and guide us. When we get ourselves into trouble, God is there, ever the loving, unselfish Parent who bails us out and turns our casualties into growth experiences, our weeping to joy, our ashes to roses.

Unless we take our fill of God's antidotes daily, we may awaken one morning and find ourselves solidly ensconced in the tradition and culture of what looks like a Christian life. In truth, however, we will have once again imprisoned our true selves in yet another faulty shell that seeks to separate us from the loving presence of God.

The danger lessens as we become more accepting and familiar with the new self and are able to accept God's strength as our own. As with any new creature, the first few weeks or years are shaky, but then as we grow into ourselves, we become more self-assured and confident. We develop integrity.

Gaining Integrity

Integrity means being complete, whole, unimpaired, competent, intact, honest, and sincere. To have integrity is to know the self and to respect each facet of the personality as well as the body, mind, and spirit. Without this integration, we have dis-integration. In order to gain integrity we must integrate all of the aspects of our being into the new self: We must pull ourselves together.

In gaining integrity we develop a strong and positive self-identity and a healthy self-esteem. Dr. William Kirwan states that "self-identity is basically each person's answer to the question 'Who am I?'" Adam and Eve, he says, "had a clear sense of their own being, or self-hood."[4]

Dr. Kirwan has developed a diagram depicting the integrated self before the fall and the broken or divided self after the fall.

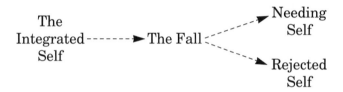

I have added the second part of Kirwan's illustration to show what we can become through Christ's restorative work within us.

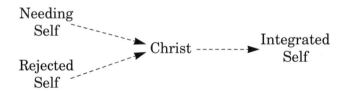

Through Christ we can be complete and integrated once again. As Kirwan says, "The deficiencies of the needing self are filled when we become God's adopted children, when we can cry, '*Abba,* Father' (Rom. 8:15–17). And the fears of the rejected self can be laid to rest because for those in Christ there is no condemnation nor separation from His love" (Rom. 8:1, 39).

The answer to "Who am I?" doesn't automatically come to us the moment Christ restores us. The answer more often comes in spurts and insightful moments as we get to know the self we've kept hidden away for so long. Because we are unique, we will not all come to know ourselves in the same way. I have found, however, in looking at my own journey and those of various Christian friends, that there tends to be a process. But the end results are much the same—a deeper self-awareness and acceptance; a love for God, self, and others; and a deep, consuming passion to be one with God and to fulfill his purpose.

I hope that you have come to accept that you were once broken, but through Christ you are a new creature: You have changed. You no longer need a shell to protect you. If the new you is to grow and mature into a whole, integrated, healthy, and holy person, you will want to learn how to work with God as you explore various facets of the new you, determine who you are, and discover the purpose for your being. In the next few chapters, we'll do just that.

11

Making New Commitments

As we saw in the last chapter, losing David to divorce shattered Marla. Their mutual friend, Ted, offered her comfort and support. "I'd have fallen apart if he hadn't been there," Marla admits. "Ted was a rock. He didn't pressure me into a relationship or anything—he was just there. He held my hand during my marathon tear sessions. He kept telling me I was beautiful and that David had been a fool for being unfaithful to me.

"It took me two years to come to grips with what had happened. Ted was so sweet. I knew he wanted to be more than a friend, but he just waited and kept saying, 'When you're ready, let me know.' And one day I knew. I'd put the past to rest. I felt a release in my spirit. I felt healed, whole, and ready to move ahead."

Ted was right to wait until Marla had become more fully healed. Had she tried to enter an intimate relationship with Ted, she may have made promises she couldn't keep. Although she grew to love him, commitment had to wait until she could offer him her whole new and healed self.

When the divorce between your new self and the old is finalized; when you have properly grieved and have come to accept the new creature you have become; when you are growing real and integrating the various parts of yourself—then you are ready for the next step in living whole. Like Marla, perhaps you are ready to make new commitments.

God encourages, loves, supports, and comforts us. He waits, never pushing, yet is always there. God yearns for a deeper, more intimate relationship with us. He hopes that once we are ready, we will commit ourselves to him. God wants more than dates where we meet him at church for a couple of hours on Sunday. God wants more than a casual affair. He wants a marriage in which we offer ourselves completely to him.

Developing a Relationship with God

Developing a new relationship takes time and effort and should not be entered into lightly. When you want to get to know someone better, you spend time with him or her. We get to know God through prayer, meditation, and by reading Scripture. The Bible tells us how God feels about us and gives us valuable insight as to what our role in this new relationship is.

When Ron and I were dating, our relationship deepened as we spent greater amounts of time together and learned more about one another. We talked about our backgrounds and personalities. I wanted to know how he felt about me. How serious was he? What did he expect from our relationship? Was I valuable to him as a person? What were his intentions? Did he love me? Did I love him enough to commit my entire life to him?

Seeing Ourselves in God's Eyes

The Bible lets us know how God sees us, how much he values us. We are new creatures created in God's image, with intellect, the ability to communicate and procreate, and to rule over the earth. We are entrusted with power to make our own choices in life (Gen. 1:26–30).

God thinks about us and nurtures us. Having designed us to be just a little lower than himself, God crowns us with glory and majesty, and has put all things under our feet (Ps. 8:4–6).

God has adopted us and offers eternal life with him in heaven. In sacrificial love he sent his Son to save us from eternal damnation. So that we would not be left to fight evil alone, God sent his Spirit to unite with our spirits to guide and comfort us (John 14:1–3, 16). To help us battle the evil still ruling the world, God even sends angels to watch over us (Heb. 1:14).

Being What God Wants Us to Be

Scripture gives proof of God's love and his desire for fellowship with us. Yet as much as God loves and values us, there can be no relationship unless we do our part. Earlier I mentioned the importance of accepting Christ's work on the cross as a means of reconciling us with the Father. But relationship is more than acceptance and acknowledgment. Just as the Bible tells us how God feels toward us, it also tells us what God requires of us. Relationship with God means we must:

- Remain faithful. "You shall have no other gods before Me" (Exod. 20:3). God is to be the number-one priority in our lives. That doesn't mean we neglect our other responsibilities, but that our relationship with God is evident in everything we think, do, and are.

- Be holy. "You shall be Holy; for I am Holy" (Lev. 11:44). As we've discovered, being holy is being whole, but it also means being set apart for God's purpose. When we are holy, we are forgiven and purified, ready instruments for whatever task God has in mind.
- Pursue righteousness. "So you will walk in the way of good men [and women] and keep to the paths of righteousness" (Prov. 2:20).
- Love. "Love the LORD your God with all your heart, and with all your soul, and with all your might" (Deut. 6:5). "Love your neighbor as yourself" (Lev. 19:18).

Perhaps you looked at this list and said, "I can't possibly be all that God wants me to be." In our own strength, these attributes are impossible to attain because they demand perfection. We must remember, however, that God knows what we are, yet can build his character within us.

The prophet Isaiah experienced the magnitude of God's power when he was called to ministry: "I saw the Lord sitting on a throne high and lifted up, and the train of His robe filled the temple. Above it stood seraphim, . . . and one cried to another and said, 'Holy, holy, holy is the LORD of hosts; the whole earth is full of His glory!' And the posts of the door were shaken by the voice of him who cried out, and the house was filled with smoke" (Isa. 6:1–4 NKJV).

Isaiah was shaken to the core by the awesome power and majesty of his God. "Woe is me," he cried, "for I am undone! Because I am a man of unclean lips, and I dwell in the midst of a people of unclean lips; for my eyes have seen the King, the LORD of Hosts" (Isa. 6:5 NKJV).

In the presence of God Isaiah melted. He saw how filthy he was compared to God, and was completely humbled. One of the seraphim touched Isaiah's mouth with a hot coal (symbolic of a purifying fire) saying, "Behold, this has touched your lips; your iniquity is taken away, and your sin is purged" (Isa. 6:7 NKJV).

At this point Isaiah heard the Lord's voice saying, "Whom shall I send, and who will go for Us?" Isaiah responded, "Here am I! Send me" (Isa. 6:8).

God cleansed Isaiah and the prophet responded instantly. His focus shifted from what he couldn't do himself to what God could do through him. Isaiah gave himself to God, and God then sent him on a vital mission.

Each of us, if we are serious about a relationship with God, must come, like Isaiah, to see the awesome power and glory of the Creator and to be utterly humbled and even melted by it.

Giving Ourselves to God

In *My Utmost for His Highest,* Oswald Chambers says we must "keep to the point." There is only one way to save ourselves, and that is to give all that we are to God. "I am determined to be absolutely and entirely for Him and for Him alone."[1]

"How can I give myself entirely to God?" you may be asking. "What does it mean?" The answer lies, in part, in a word many have come to dislike: *submission.*

We must lay aside our pride, our fears, and our own desires and allow God to mold us. Submission is difficult for many of us. If you struggle with this concept, perhaps it is because you are still broken. One of the symptoms of brokenness is the need to maintain control over ourselves and others. We expend vast amounts of energy maintaining the status quo. Our greatest fear is letting go, afraid God might make us do something we don't want to do.

For many, however, submission may be difficult because we don't fully understand what the term means. Satan would like us to believe that submission means letting another person control us.

I've heard some religious leaders insist that submission

requires that we set aside our own agendas and give up everything, even our identities and sense of being, to God, to the church, or to a mate.

Something inside us furiously resists being controlled. I'm reminded of a story I once heard about Amy, a little girl who loved to draw. Her parents encouraged her and supplied their budding artist with colors and paints and reams of paper.

Then one day Amy went off to school. The teacher smiled and said, "Today, boys and girls, we're going to learn how to draw flowers." Amy eagerly pulled out her colors and sketch pad and began to draw.

"What do you think you're doing?" the teacher asked, frowning. "That's not the way we draw flowers." She snatched Amy's drawing, tore it in half, and threw it away. "From now on, you'll listen to my instructions. This," she said, drawing an oval on the board, "is how we draw flowers."

Amy's first impulse was to resist. Then she remembered what her parents had said. "Be a good girl. Do what your teacher says." So Amy did.

A year later, another teacher told the class that it was drawing day. Amy waited for the instructions. Seeing that her student wasn't drawing, the teacher asked, "What's wrong, Amy? Why aren't you drawing?"

Amy sighed. "I don't know how," she said. "You have to show me."

Tragically, Amy submitted to her first teacher and lost an important part of herself, her ability to create beautiful pictures. Perhaps we, too, fear that submission to authority could cause us to lose ourselves. And we are right to be wary.

On the other hand, in order to be whole and healthy, we need to be submitted to God. We need God's steady hand in our lives; we need his boundaries and instruction. So what do we do?

In the struggle to maintain our identities, we may become like rebellious children, insisting on our own way. Many may fight control because they have been victims of oppressive relationships. Even though we know the word *control* does not always have a negative connotation, we may bristle at the thought. Letting someone else, even God, control us, often feels utterly wrong. I've struggled with this issue time and again. I resist being controlled. Is this wrong?

It seems to me that submitting to God and to others does not mean we stop being ourselves. It doesn't mean that we allow others to overpower us. As we saw in Amy's case, an overbearing teacher robbed Amy of her creativity. The truth is, we were never meant to be controlled or victimized. And God does not want to imprison us, he wants us to experience freedom. He desires our company and wants us to be all that he created us to be. God wants us to partake of his goodness; he wants to be our divine counselor, our nurturing, loving parent.

Wanting a more expert opinion on the subject, I called a pastor friend. "You're right," she said, when I shared my views. "God never forces us, we must invite him. Look at Revelation 3:20 where the Lord says, 'Behold, I stand at the door and knock. If anyone hears My voice and opens the door, I will come in to him and dine with him, and he with me.' Jesus offers us a place with him on the throne. That doesn't sound like control to me."

My friend went on to say that she sees the element of control in evil, not in love. "Many cult leaders, for example, exercise control—they wield their power over the mindless masses and demand submission. Demonic spirits are very controlling. They want to take possession of our bodies, minds, and souls. God isn't like that."

We might also want to look at the Scripture defining perfect love. In 1 Corinthians 13:5 we're told that "Love does not insist on its own way." Rather than control us, God desires us to freely give him our selves and our devotion.

If I might use the analogy, our relationship to God is much like that between a husband and wife. Ideally they will both willingly submit their bodies to one another in mutual love and respect. If either manipulates, controls, or uses force, he or she is abusing the other. If God were to force himself on us it would be spiritual rape. The God I've come to know in my heart and in the pages of the Bible would never do that.

God is not controlling, but relational. When we offer ourselves to him, we move from a state of immature dependence (where we must rely solely on others outside of God for our existence), and/or independence (where we rely solely on ourselves), to *interdependence* (where we share a mutual dependence). In interdependence we offer all that we are to God and he offers himself to us. We work with him to accomplish his purpose. We do this, not out of fear that he will punish us if we don't, but out of love and reverence, trusting that God knows and wants to meet our every need.

Christians are not to be whiny, cowering, fearful, or spineless victims caught in a web of confusion and deceit. We are to be strong (Eph. 6:10; Heb. 11:34); bold in spirit (Eph. 3:12); determined to lovingly and joyfully serve God and humanity (Gal. 5:13; Col. 3:24; Heb. 9:14); run the race with endurance (Heb. 12:1); strive for excellence and wisdom, and press on toward the goal of becoming whole (holy) and Christ-like (Phil. 3:14). God wants us to freely come to him. As Ron Mehl, author of *Surprise Endings* says, "Without us, God will not, and without God, we cannot."

Submitting to God may at times be an uncomfortable and even painful process, but it does not diminish us in any way. We retain our talents and abilities, our personalities and character traits. We may, and in fact, we must lose the old self, but the new creation is enhanced as we give ourselves up to God's care. With our permission, God will fill us with himself, enhance, strengthen, and empower us in ways we never imagined (Eph. 3:19–20).

As I mentioned earlier, my son was a strong-willed child. He always insisted on doing things his way. It was as though he feared that submitting to his parents would take all the fun out of life.

As a parent, though, I never really wanted to control my son. I only wanted him to change direction so that he could experience joy and happiness rather than the misery into which I knew he was headed. I wanted to assist him in making decisions that would enhance his life. I would have been thrilled if he had simply submitted to walking with me, if we could have listened to one another and shared ideas and dreams. I would have been delighted to watch him grow and develop into a mature adult.

God has given us freedom to choose the kind of life we want to live. When we submit to God, he doesn't take that freedom from us. Rather, God embraces us and shows us how we can live life to the fullest. As the perfect parent, he gives us guidelines and shows us the boundaries. He tells us the consequences of our immoral choices and leaves the decisions to us.

Perhaps you've decided to submit to God. You realize God's way is far better than your way. "But," you may be asking, "how do we submit to God?" the answer lies, in part, in one of the most enigmatic statements Jesus ever made: "Assuredly, I say to you, whoever does not receive the kingdom of God as a little child will by no means enter it" (Mark 10:15 NKJV).

How can we do this? Let's move into the next chapter and find out.

12

As Little Children

ISAIAH CAME TO GOD AS A CHILD. He was overwhelmed by God's power and ability, eager to please, and absolutely trusting. There is something fresh and innocent and almost magical about children. I am continually amazed at the wisdom that comes from children who are allowed to express themselves.

For example, one day while Corisa, then three, and I were playing in the park, I gave her a push on the swing. Wondering why she seemed so delighted, I asked, "What's swinging like?"

She cocked her head and thought for a moment, and then replied, "Nanna, it's like a summer day."

Most of us enjoy watching children and take delight in what they say and do. Nevertheless, the idea of becoming like a child may not have much appeal to you. Perhaps that's because as adults, we think of returning to child-likeness as regression. But it needn't be. In fact, becoming like children is a progression into a more mature faith. It is a regaining of territory that was lost in our shell-building years.

To more fully understand what it means to become like children, we need to adjust our attitudes. We may need to rethink our ideas on what being an adult, and what being a child, really mean.

Child-development specialist Erik Erikson theorized that children, in order to develop into mature, healthy adults, needed to first gain a sense of trust, and then autonomy.

At first we may presume the children are gaining something they never had. But I wonder. Isn't it possible that children are born with an innate sense of trust and autonomy, and that life in a broken world erodes these inbred qualities and keeps them from developing in the healthy ways God intended?

As we grow and develop into adulthood, we lose our sense of wonder and exchange childhood trust and autonomy for adult paranoia and dependence. We lose our integrity and dis-integrate.

A Sense of Wonder

Have you ever taken time to experience the imagination of a child? My friend Gail recently shared a story about her daughter, Marla, as a small child. Gail and her husband were driving home with Marla one night when they heard an alarmed cry from the back seat. "Oh, no! Look, the moon is broken!" The adults looked up to where the tiny finger pointed. There in the night sky hung a narrow sliver of a moon, where only a few days ago it had been whole.

Before they could explain about moon shadows, Marla sighed and said, "Oh well, that's all right. My daddy will fix it." In a child's mind anything can happen and often does: Daddies can even fix the moon.

While driving cross-country with our then-two-year-old granddaughter, Hannah, my husband pointed out several herds of antelope beside the road. "Hannah," he'd say, "Look at the antelope. Can you see them?" Each time, she peered through the window but could not spot them. After a while, Hannah decided two could play this game. "Papa!" she exclaimed. "There's a red lion and a pink panther!"

Later Corisa, then four, was riding alone with me. We were philosophizing about life when she began to tell me about her "people of the eye."

"Oh," I said. "What do you mean?"

She looked at me as though this were a piece of wisdom everyone should know, then as if seeing I were just an adult, explained it to me. "People of the eye are ones you love that have to go away. But even if they're gone you can still see them when you close your eyes. Those are people of the eye."

"Wow," I said. "Did you think of that all by yourself?"

"Yes." She nodded and grinned. "I also thought about people of the nose."

Where do they come from, these wild, magical, fantastic, and imaginative thoughts? But more importantly, where do they go when we grow up, and why do so many of us leave them behind?

Author Robert Wood offers this suggestion:

> With the hardening of our categories of interpretation and goal-projection, wonder disappears from life; we become "adult," and the world becomes familiar, routine. We lose the capacity to sense the depth hidden within the simple *presence* of things; real living disappears. And when living mutually vanishes, then mistrust, curiosity, and routine step in to establish the fundamental modes of relation to others. With the disappearance of relation, religion likewise disappears.

Speculation regarding this childlike sense of wonder and what happens to it when we grow up abounds. Philosophers and theologians have debated the topic for centuries. In this century psychoanalysts have entered the debate. One of the difficulties we adults have is that we must filter what we learn about children through our adult minds. Yet, if Jesus has said we must be as children, then it must be possible to regain our sense of wonder and childlikeness. Below I discuss some of the childlike qualities we adults may need to reclaim: trust, faith, resiliency, honesty, transparency, imitation, and love.

Children Trust

Children respond to the adults in their lives with utter abandon. The other day I watched as a man set his son on a high platform. The little boy lifted his arms and threw himself into his daddy's arms. He had no fear.

Children don't worry about what they will eat or drink or what they will wear. Experience with people who don't catch them, or care for them, or meet their needs teaches mistrust. When a child's trust is broken, the child may build a shell of cynicism and doubt. The ability to trust is still within each of us, but we may have trouble seeing it because of our shells.

Once you become as a child and step free of your shell, you can begin to regain your trust. Then, even when you are naughty and test God to the limits, you will *know* God loves you and will never leave or forsake you. And you'll *know,* even when hard times crush you, that God will care for you and will always catch you when you fall, or even when you jump.

Jesus trusted God. He allowed himself to be beaten, stripped, and nailed to a cross, trusting that the Father would give him new life in the resurrection. Can we trust God that much? If we are like children, yes.

Children Believe

In like manner, children believe until the world gives them reason not to. In a child's mind anything is possible—the virgin birth and the resurrection—and even the wisdom of grandmothers. One day Corisa and I were having one of our philosophical discussions. Not yet having discovered my intellectual shortcomings, she said, "Nanna, you know everything."

I smiled (naturally), and said, "Thank you for thinking that, Honey, but only God knows everything."

She thought for a moment, and in a tone that booked no opposition, said, "You and God, Nanna, know everything."

While they may not always be entirely accurate, children often are able to grasp certain concepts adults can't fathom. Many adults have difficulty with the concept of a triune God. We speak the words of the Apostles' Creed, but do we really experience it? I think children have that ability.

My daughter and her husband recently moved to Minnesota. For several months before the actual move from Washington state, my son-in-law worked in Minnesota. During this time, he brought home a video to show the family the home he'd found for them. When Hannah, age two, saw her daddy in the video, she insisted that there were two daddies. The one on television was in Minnesota, and the other was present in the living room. He was the same daddy, one in two parts. We might, as rational adults, say that's nonsense. Certainly our brains have progressed to the point where there is no mystery in Hannah's two-daddy theory. But have we also, in gaining what we call reason, lost the ability to believe in the unreasonable? When we come to God as a child, all things are possible.

Children Are Resilient

Even severely abused children, when given over to loving, caring parents, can go on to live healthy, well-adjusted lives. Children are like soft, pliant clay. For a time they can be molded and shaped. They are resilient, unassuming, and forgiving.

Eventually, the clay hardens. As we grow, we become rigid, afraid to take chances, afraid to bend. If we become too hardened, the only way we can be changed and saved is to be broken and reformed.

Jesus, who was God, allowed himself to be formed as an embryo, and planted in a virgin's womb. Taking on human form and substance, he became like us to show us the way to wholeness. He was broken for our transgressions. His death and resurrection formed the living water that flows into our rigidity and softens us so we become pliant once more. If we become as children, we can submit and allow God to reshape us.

Children Are Honest

Have you ever noticed how honest a child can be? Gene was speeding. The red lights flashing in his rearview mirror directed him to pull over. Gene swore and muttered, "I've got a good notion to give that jerk a piece of my mind."

When the patrolman approached the car, Gene rolled down the window and smiled. "Hello officer, what's the trouble?"

"Hey, Dad," Ronnie piped up from the back seat. "Aren't you gonna give that jerk a piece of your mind like you said?"

I'm reminded of a story I once heard about a child who was frightened of the dark. Mother came in to comfort him, saying, "It's okay, Sweetheart. Jesus will keep you safe."

"I know," the little boy whimpered, "but sometimes I need somebody with skin on."

When children hurt, they cry. When they are happy, they laugh. Their emotions, as much a part of them as skin, are expressed openly and honestly—until they learn that being open is unacceptable. Telling the truth can get them into trouble—it might even cause Mom and Dad to get mad, to go away and not love them any more.

Children come into the world naked and unashamed. They learn to cover themselves. Jesus, as honest as a child, embarrassed religious leaders by revealing their hypocrisy. Jesus wept openly at the death of a friend. Enraged at what humanity had done to the temple, he tore it apart. Jesus was honest.

Children Are Transparent

Closely related to honesty is transparency. Transparency is an unguarded state, which allows others to read us. God's image, the pure self, can be seen as clearly as a light through a window. In my spirituality class at seminary, Professor Frances Whiting told this story, which to me illustrates transparency: A boy and his father visited a lavish ancient cathedral. They stood transfixed by the beauty and translucence of the figures in the stained-glass windows that lined the walls. "Daddy," the little boy whispered as he pulled on his father's arm. "Who are those people the light shines through?"

The Bible tells us to be shining lights. Sadly, as we grow older, the light is often hidden behind the darkness of our insecurities and fears. The windows become stained and dull, dirtied by sin and covered by denial.

Children Imitate

Children learn how to live by imitating the people around them. Just the other day I was playing with an infant. I smiled; he smiled. I formed an O with my mouth and opened my eyes wide; he did the same.

As new creatures, we learn and grow by imitating Christ and emulating those spiritually mature saints who have made or are making the spiritual journey to wholeness.

Children Love

I learn a great many things from children. Love is one of them. A child's love is simple, pure, and spontaneous. A child doesn't examine love from all angles and attach all kinds of labels to it. If we watch closely, children can show us what real love is.

Angie was only six when her best friend, Cassie, was killed in an automobile accident. After the funeral, Angie walked to where her friend's mother sat, climbed into her lap, and put her small, wiry arms around the woman's neck. Love flowed from Angie to Cassie's mother. Love for that moment was a little girl who filled a grieving mother's empty arms.

Most adults have been tucked inside their shells for so long they've forgotten how to love. Oswald Chambers says, "If human love does not carry [us] beyond [ourselves] it is not love. If love is always discreet, always wise, always sensible and calculating, never carried beyond itself, it is not love at all. It may be warmth of feeling, but it has not the true nature of love in it."[1]

A child's unconditional, unconscious love is hard to destroy. Even children who have been severely abused by a parent continue, at least for a time, to offer love. Perhaps they love out of fear of being abandoned. Perhaps they love because they have not yet learned to hate. Or perhaps they love because it is part of their nature.

Love, like a refreshing mountain stream, begins with God, flows into humanity, and then flows out to others. If we stop the flow, we become stagnant and rancid. Children never stop love's natural flow until we teach them how.

Jesus hung on the cross. He'd been stripped, beaten. Nails pierced his hands and feet. In these, his most agonizing moments, Jesus poured his love out to humankind as he cried, "Father, forgive them, for they do not know what they do" (Luke 23:34). Could there be a greater love than this?

Love allows us to abandon ourselves to God, as a child

to a loving parent. We hand God all our misguided beliefs, our lack of trust, dishonesty, inflexibility, and warped love, and he replaces them with the real thing.

Consequently, we no longer need to validate ourselves through false images because our realness is found in the true self, bearing God's image. Being whole is loving who we are and loving the God who created us—unconditionally. Wholeness gives us freedom to love God with all of our heart, soul, and strength (Deut. 6:4).

Just as a child is validated by a parent's love and acceptance, we, too, are validated and made complete in God's love. We love because God first loved us. Since God's love is unconditional, nothing we do can diminish it. There are no limitations. We do not gain God's love by what we do. We are loved simply because we are. When God's love is allowed to flow unhindered, we relearn how to love with no limits, requirements, or expectations. To God we are priceless. Nothing kept God from doing what was necessary to restore our relationship with him. God knows what we need.

Martin Luther once said, "I have held many things in my hands and I have lost them all; but whatever I have placed in God's hands, that I still possess." Let us then place ourselves in God's hands, knowing that in the process we will not lose ourselves, but find our true selves.

As we deepen our relationship with God, we are called to make a commitment to him. Some of you may have already done this, but some may still be holding back. Are you willing to become as a child and give yourself to God? The cost of commitment is great, but so are the rewards.

Coming to God as a child allows us to regain the wonder of life and of God. As a delighted parent, God encourages us to grow and develop in healthy ways, to use our God-given talents and abilities. He empowers us to use our skills and gifts to build up others as well as ourselves.

Discovering the Child in You

For the next few minutes, think about the children you know. How is living in a broken world affecting them?

Think about what you were like as a child. Can you remember a time when you trusted completely, when you were sure of yourself and of God? Do you remember ever loving without ulterior motives? What qualities have you lost? Would you like to become like a child again?

Write these thoughts in your journal. Pray that God will heal the hurts and scars from childhood wounds. Ask him to restore in you those childlike qualities that will allow you to become Christ-like.

There is more to being a child than regaining those natural qualities that help us to better relate to God. The healthiest children are those who have loving parental supervision. Caring parents help their children gain integrity, a sense of self-esteem and purpose. They know the importance of obedience, submission, and self-discipline. In the next chapters we'll discuss these developmental traits as they relate to re-parenting the child in us.

13

Having
a Sense of Purpose

I RECENTLY WATCHED A NEWS PROGRAM about a study of people over one hundred years of age. In studying these centenarians, doctors found four common threads linking their longevity:

- Activity: maintaining a lifestyle that keeps the mind and body moving. One 105-year-old woman led an exercise program every morning. Another, at 104, worked as a guide in a historic home.
- Commitment: being involved in a cause. One man plays an active role in his church, attending services twice a week. His faith sustains him.
- Positive attitude: smiling, laughing, being able to find joy and purpose in life regardless of the sorrow.
- Resiliency: the ability to bounce back, to deal with loss and overcome depression.

Each of these people displayed a sense of integrity—of knowing who they are, being comfortable with and at peace with themselves, and having a clear sense of purpose. We can have these qualities as well, and don't have to wait until we're a hundred to attain them.

Earlier I discussed becoming integrated, or whole. An important part of this process is knowing more fully who we are and where we belong.

Integrity Is Knowing Your Purpose

Part of being fully integrated is having a strong sense of purpose and belonging. It is knowing your areas of gift-edness—what you are good at and what you do best—knowing your strengths and weaknesses. When we have integrity, we recognize our potential. We not only accept talents and abilities as gifts from God, we allow God to use them for his purpose.

Knowing these things about ourselves prevents us from wasting valuable time trying to be something we are not. One of the keys to gaining integrity is to study the gifts and learn which are ours. In Romans 12:3–13, Paul tells us how to use spiritual gifts.

We are not to think of ourselves more highly than we ought, but to consider seriously what God has dealt us according to the faith we have. Just as there are many parts to our physical bodies, there are many members of the body of Christ (the church). We have different functions and duties, but we belong to one another and need one another in order to function well. Having then gifts differing according to the grace that is given us to, *let us use them:*

- Prophecy, *let us prophesy* (speak out for God) in proportion to our faith (as God enables)
- Ministry, (meeting other's needs) *let us use it in our ministering*

- One who teaches, in teaching
- One who exhorts (urges, counsels, and advises), in exhortation
- One who gives should do so liberally
- Those with leadership abilities are to lead with diligence, not for personal gain, but as a service to others
- Those who show mercy are to offer compassion and empathy with cheerfulness

Paul also tells us we are to love without hypocrisy, hate evil, hold tight to what is good, be affectionate, and give honor to one another. Further, we are to embrace life and serve God with diligence and passion, as we rejoice in hope, show patience in tribulation, earnestly offer prayer, and meet the needs of others.

Learning Who You Are

How do we discover who we are? Fortunately, we have many tools for self-discovery, including personality tests and spiritual giftedness inventories.

A Personality Profile

In my quest to gain integrity and wholeness, I first spent time trying to get to know and understand myself. I began by allowing the new creature in me more freedom to explore and found her to be much bolder than the old me. Part of that exploration involved taking a number of temperament and personality inventories. The first was in Florence Littauer's book *Personality Plus.* I found I was both a dreamer—fun-loving, creative, adventurous, disorganized—and at the same time serious—deep, analytical, and orderly. This wasn't an easy mix to deal with, but I appreciated having traits I had always questioned in myself explained. Later I took the Myers-Briggs Type Indicator, which depicted me as a highly intuitive introvert, a deep thinker, creative and caring.

What matters here is not so much keying into the specific aspects of our personalities, but embracing the idea that it's okay to be ourselves. When we see that we do not all have the same temperament or personality, we no longer need to re-create a shell-like self that we think will be pleasing to others. We no longer need to imitate others' personalities in order to fit in. Personality inventories can help us understand and accept ourselves and others.

Spiritual Giftedness

I also read several books on finding and using spiritual gifts, and I began to understand where I fit in—my purpose.

One of my favorites was a book by Marcia Mitchell entitled *Giftedness.* I completed a questionnaire to determine what my spiritual gifts were and scored highest in the areas of counseling, exhortation, teaching, and mercy.

The outcome strongly affirmed the new creature in me, who cared about others and enjoyed counseling, writing, speaking, and teaching. Knowing what gifts God has given me adds cohesiveness to my ministry. Instead of wishing I were like this person or that, I'm content to be who I am.

Not knowing who we are or what our purpose is can lead to a great deal of frustration, as this parable shows:

> Once upon a time, the animals decided to organize a new school. They adopted a curriculum of running, climbing, swimming, and flying. To make it easier to administer the curriculum, all the animals took all the subjects.
>
> The duck excelled in swimming. He swam even better than his instructor. He made only passing grades in flying, however, and was a very poor runner. In order to improve his running skills, he had to drop swimming and stay after school to run. His lovely webbed feet became badly worn

from running, which dropped his grade in swimming to a
"C." But average was quite acceptable, so nobody worried
about that—except the duck.

The rabbit started out at the top of her class in running,
but developed a nervous twitch in her leg muscles because
she had to do so much makeup work in swimming.

The squirrel surpassed all of them in climbing, but
encountered constant frustration in flying class because
his teacher insisted he start from the ground up instead of
from the treetop down. He developed "charlie horses" from
overexertion, and ended up with a "C" in climbing and a
"D" in running.

The eagle was a problem child. Her teachers severely
disciplined her for being a nonconformist. In climbing
classes she beat all the others to the top of the tree, but
insisted on using her own way to get there.[1]

If you're unsure of your unique talents or personality
traits, I encourage you to read books like those I mentioned
to help you better understand who and why you are.

Along with discovering your gifts, you may want to note
in your journal some of the different characteristics you
see in yourself. List your interests, your hobbies, your character qualities, and your strengths and weaknesses. Get
to know who you are.

When the World Says No

One of the tragedies we face in our brokenness is that
once we discover what we believe to be our purpose, we may
be thwarted by people whose personal biases may cause
them to say that we can't be what we feel called to be.

I think especially of one woman pastor. Even though she
is gifted in preaching, she has been restrained by people
who have a different interpretation of freedom through
Christ. When my friend Ann applied for internship in her
church she was told, "You can intern here, you just can't

preach." How foolish. And this church, on paper, at least, ordains women.

Parents may push their children into vocations they are not suited for and don't desire. Men and women are sometimes expected to fill traditional roles that do not necessarily match up with their personalities or spiritual gifts.

Knowing your purpose, knowing your areas of giftedness, and understanding who you are can give you courage to move away from your shell and into a world where you can be true to your calling. And yes, you do have a calling or a purpose. Oswald Chambers says, "The call of God is not for the special few, it is for everyone. Whether or not I hear God's call depends upon the state of my ears; and what I hear depends on my disposition."[2]

The Call of God

As you move from discovering who you are and where you fit to having a sense of purpose and being called of God, you now need to back off from your findings. While it is good to know about ourselves and our gifts, we'll want to be careful not to attach too much importance to them. Personality tests give us data that can help us identify strengths and weaknesses and better understand how we relate to one another, but they cannot offer a complete assessment of who, what, and why we are. Our purpose is not dependent on our perceptions of self, but on God's perception of us. Set aside your own ideas and dreams and listen to God.

"The call of God," Chambers says, "is not the echo of my nature; my affinities and personal temperament are not considered. As long as I consider my personal temperament and think about what I am fitted for, I shall never hear the call of God."[3] We come, not filled with a sense of our own importance or plans, but with the sense of awe that Isaiah experienced in God's presence. When Isaiah heard God's call, he did not respond out of an arrogant, self-oriented attitude of "I'm talented in this area; surely I can do great things for God." Rather, he responded with amazement and humility: "I am nothing, but here I am, send me." About the calling of God, Chambers goes on to say, "The majority of us have no ear for anything but ourselves, we cannot hear a thing God says."

Knowing ourselves can be a good thing, but we must take care that our self-awareness does not create yet another egocentric shell that will prevent us from hearing and answering God's call.

New Life

Once we discard the shell and embrace the new creatures we are becoming, we'll find that the egg we once were has been changed. We've hatched, and under God's care, are growing more mature every day. When the time is right and we have adjusted to our new selves and gained integrity, God will teach us how to fly.

I'm reminded of the beautiful promise in Isaiah 40:31: "But they that wait on the LORD shall renew their strength; they shall mount up with wings like eagles, they shall run and not be weary, they shall walk and not faint" (NKJV).

The Lord nudges us out of the nest, which can be scary but, at the same time, challenging and exciting. For me, flight meant entering a new career as a writer and speaker in midlife. It meant enrolling in graduate school at age forty-four to pursue a degree in counseling.

Have you taken any flights lately? If you have discarded your shell and become a new creature, be assured it will happen. When it does, I encourage you to go. My life has changed completely since my first flight. There have been many fearful moments, but the joy of flying far outweighs the difficulties.

The Old Testament tells us that three months after the exodus from Egypt, the children of Israel were camped in the wilderness. The Lord said to Moses, "You have seen what I did to the Egyptians [the enemy], and how I bore you up on eagles' wings and brought you to Myself. Now therefore, if you will indeed obey My voice and keep My covenant, then you shall be a special treasure to Me above all people; for the earth is Mine. And you shall be to Me a kingdom of priests and a holy nation" (Exod. 19:4–6 NKJV).

We, too, can be God's special treasures, a kingdom of priests, when we allow him to bear us up on eagles' wings and lead us away from our old shells and the influence of evil. We shall be one with God and we shall be whole (holy).

14

Life
in the Garden

RECENTLY MY HUSBAND AND I visited Epcot Center in Orlando, Florida. Since I'd been there before, I was able to suggest a route that would take us through the most interesting exhibits. I was able to guide my husband in the same way a friend had guided me my first time there.

When we visit a historic site or a museum, the experience is often made more meaningful by a knowledgeable tour guide. Coming into the Garden and experiencing real Christianity can be even more overwhelming than entering a theme park for the first time. Like little children, newcomers to the Garden need someone to guide them, teach them, and show them where to go and what to see.

We can find guidance by studying the lives of those who have gone before us and by seeking out mentors. At this stage it is tempting to make a long list of things you can do to live a holy and healthy life, but it is not that simple. Certain behaviors can enhance our journey to wholeness, but in the end everything depends on our personal ability

168

to relate to God, on how clearly we hear his voice, and on how willing we are to change.

As I've studied the writings and lives of godly men and women, I am struck by their desire to strive for truth and know God in a more intimate way. I am also encouraged as they reveal their brokenness and subsequent healing through Christ. One trait these saints share is an ability to listen to God.

Listening to God

We hear God when our spirits are in tune with his. Unfortunately, the world's cries and demands are often so loud we can't always be certain whose voice we're hearing. We need to listen to what God is saying through his Word.

One of these saints I've studied under, Dr. Bill Vermillion, a professor at Western Evangelical Seminary said, "Rather than study the Bible, let it study you." We tend to talk too much and listen too little. In the Bible God speaks to us when we open our hearts and listen. Part of listening is asking, "What is Jesus saying to me personally in this passage?"

When you read the Bible, make your study personal.

1. Read the passage several times.
2. Circle key concepts.
3. Write down (in a journal) a truth you've discovered.
4. Express your need in that area.
5. Answer these questions: What does it mean to me? How does it affect my life today?

The Bible is truly the living Word. As Martin Luther said, "The Bible is alive . . . it speaks to me . . . it has feet . . . it runs after me . . . it has hands . . . it lays hold on me."

We can also listen to God in prayer and meditation, and we will be discussing these shortly.

Listening to God can be threatening, so we listen to preachers and friends, but seldom to God. To humans we can say no, but when we listen to God and he speaks, the message is so clear that we can't ignore it. God's voice compels us, and our spirits won't let us walk away. Oswald Chambers says, "The call of God can never be stated explicitly; it is implicit. . . . like the call of the sea, no one hears it but the one who has the nature of the sea in him [or her]."[1]

Consider how you will respond to God when he calls you to a task. How willing are you to submit yourself to God? How willing are you to be used in ministry? Can you really do God's will rather than your own? Can you truly submit yourself and let Jesus be Lord of your life with all that entails? In his book *James,* Harold L. Fickett Jr. tells of a British woman who said, "I want the Lord to be my Constitutional King, but I want to be Prime Minister."[2]

While the king is the figurehead with limited authority, the prime minister rules. So it is all too often with us. We give Jesus a crown, while our demanding self-will makes all the decisions.

Taking Inventory

Another quality I see in healed and whole people is an awareness of themselves and the ability to honestly assess their lives. In order to maintain a healthy relationship with our new selves and with God, it is necessary to do routine personal inventories. Periodically ask yourself these questions:

- Do I experience the fruit of the Spirit? "But the fruit of the Spirit is love, joy, peace, longsuffering, kindness, goodness, faithfulness, gentleness, self-control" (Gal. 5:22–23 NKJV).

- Am I at peace with my family and myself?
- Am I involved with other people who love God and are centered in him?
- Am I content regardless of my circumstances?
- Do I love unconditionally?
- Do I truly love the Lord with all my heart, mind, and soul, and my neighbor as myself?
- Am I free to be intimate with God?
- Am I free to be intimate with others?

Forgiving As You Are Forgiven

Another saintly quality and a very important part of maintaining a relationship with God is being sensitive to wrongdoing. The Lord's Prayer tells us to ask for forgiveness for our own sins, and then to forgive others. When we are close to someone, we know instinctively when we have done something to hurt them. The wrong puts a wedge between us and creates an uncomfortable tension. In healthy relationships, the partners communicate.

"I'm sorry, I was wrong," does not roll off my lips easily. I struggle with it and try to volley the blame into the other person's court like a tennis ball. Eventually, if I value the relationship enough, I'll admit my mistakes.

When we are in partnership with God, it is doubly hard to ask forgiveness. God is never wrong. If the relationship seems to be faltering, we have to look at ourselves, not God, for the root of the problem. I'm still in the process of learning to set aside my pride and come to God the moment I feel myself slipping away.

Once we ask forgiveness, we need to be able to live as though we're forgiven. Holding on to that which God has let go of is in a sense saying, "God I don't believe you." God doesn't hold grudges. To forgive means to give forth, to send away. Dr. Francis Whiting, one of my seminary professors, told us this story as an example of this concept.

> A pastor of a certain church felt deep concern over Kathy, a ten-year-old girl in his congregation, who claimed that Jesus actually talked to her. The pastor tried to ignore her but felt her insistence went beyond simple childhood imaginings. Kathy seemed well adjusted otherwise, but the pastor thought perhaps she needed counseling.
>
> Finally, he went to the bishop in his area and explained the matter to him. The bishop thought for a moment, then said, "Why don't we simply test this out. See whether or not her claims are real. Ask Kathy to ask Jesus what the bishop said in his last confession. Only Jesus will know that."
>
> The pastor did as the bishop suggested and Kathy agreed to ask Jesus about the bishop.
>
> A few days later the pastor talked with Kathy and said, "Well, tell me what Jesus said when you asked him about the bishop's confession."
>
> Kathy replied, "Jesus said to tell you that he's forgotten."

We need to believe that God's forgiveness is complete and ask God to make our forgiveness of others and of ourselves complete as well.

People who have journeyed from brokenness to wholeness have the ability to forgive. They also have an inner strength that makes them resilient and strong enough to face whatever crisis they may encounter.

Being Strong

Do we have enough strength and health to withstand difficulty? Our bodies are equipped with certain blood cells that rush in to save us from offending bacteria. These healthy cells literally engulf and eat the offending attackers. In our spiritual lives, are we strong enough to destroy the offending spirits and survive the difficulties and hard times? Do we allow God's strength—his Spirit—to equip us to do warfare against the princes and principalities of darkness?

As reconciled and restored individuals, we have not been given "a spirit of fear, but of power and of love and of a sound mind" (2 Tim. 1:7 NKJV). Let's not be afraid to challenge, to ask questions, to fight for what we know is God's will. Let's not be afraid to face all manner of evil that surrounds us and fight to the death, if we must, for what we believe to be the truth. And finally, let's release God from our stained-glass prisons, from artificial rules and barriers, and from stiff definitions of what faith should be. Let's open wide the doors of our imaginations and let God be God. Let God rip away all pretense and every façade— every shell fragment that keeps us from being whole. And let us face life strengthened by the armor of God.

Keeping a Journal

Early in the book I encouraged you to keep a journal. It's a practice you may want to continue. Many of the more mature Christians I've known write about their experiences, answered prayers, and thoughts in journals. Sometimes when the difficulties of the world are more than we can bear, it is hard to see what God has done for us. At times like these we can find hope and courage if we take a trip back through the pages of a journal and review where we have been. We often need to be reminded of what God has accomplished in our lives.

Keeping a journal can help you do that. In it, write your testimony, your intimate talks with God, and events from your spiritual journey, and you'll be able to see more clearly how you have traveled from brokenness to healing and how you are being transformed.

Nourishing Your Soul

A common trait I see in mature Christians is the diligent manner in which they nurture their souls. If we are to grow and stand fast in our faith, we must provide our souls with food. Study the Bible and Bible commentaries and take a Bible-study course or a theology class at a Christian college or seminary. Fill your soul with the inspirational works of writers such as Augustine, Andrew Murray, C. S. Lewis, Henri Nouwen, St. Teresa of Avila, John Wesley, Hannah Whitall Smith, and Oswald Chambers. Read contemporary books such as *The Celebration of Discipline* by Richard Foster, *No Wonder They Call Him Savior* by Max Lucado, or *While Walking on Water I Sank* by Joe Lomuscio.

And indulge your soul with music, art, and beauty. The classics can fill you and make you weep. The arts—whether we're creating our own masterpieces or admiring the work done by others—can remind us of God's powerful presence in each of us.

Enjoy and care for the earth. See God's majesty in the ocean and the mountains. See his wisdom in snowflakes. And see his delight in the laughter of a child.

Meditation and Prayer

A common thread among those who live whole (holy) lives is that they spend time with God in meditation and prayer. Unfortunately, our desire and ability to spend time alone with God often gets shuffled to the bottom of our things-to-do lists. Jacques Ellul, author of *Prayer and the Modern Man,* writes:

> The man of our time does not know how to pray; but much more than that, he has neither the desire nor the need to do so. He does not find the deep source of prayer within himself. I am acquainted with him well. It is myself.[3]

Some Christians avoid meditation, fearing that the art is somehow an evil representation of a false religion. This is another of Satan's ploys to separate us from God and rob us of the joy that basking in God's Presence can bring. The Bible clearly indicates God's desire for our attention. For example, in Joshua 4:8, the Lord said, "This Book of the Law shall not depart from your mouth, but you shall meditate in it day and night." When we meditate we dwell on God, his works, and his Word.

Another hindrance to meditation is lack of time. We often get so busy with life that we don't take time for God. We avoid the very essence of intimacy with God. Meditating requires silence, concentration, discipline, and time. Our busy lives don't allow it. If meditation and prayer are difficult for you, here are some tips that may help:

1. Set aside twenty to thirty minutes a day (at least) listening to, loving, and talking with God.
2. Slow down. Concentrate on relaxing your entire body. A body and mind at rest can more easily get in touch with God's presence within.
3. Read St. Teresa of Avila's *A Life of Prayer*. It will change your life. Dr. Clayton L. Berg Jr., the editor of Teresa's work on prayer, wrote:

   > Prayer for Teresa is much more than just "saying our prayers." It is God giving Himself and we receiving Him. Thus, when we are really in earnest, steadily pursuing God's will, in an attitude of faith and an act of trust and commitment, it will not be long before we are blessed by His life-giving touch.
   >   . . . Teresa calls us with great urgency to have communion with God. "Souls without prayer are like people whose bodies or limbs are paralyzed: they possess feet and hands but they cannot control them."

4. Don't give up your time alone with God. Satan continually works to keep our focus on everything but

God. We are caught up in the things of this world: We are too busy *doing* and not taking time to *be*. Martin Luther said, "I have so much to do I must spend four hours in meditation and prayer instead of two."

5. Through meditation we receive assurance, peace, joy, and patience. We give our hearts, minds, and emotions a chance to rest in God's arms.
6. Come into the Garden and let God minister to you beside the still waters.

One of my most insightful lessons about taking time out came, naturally, from a child. My friend Jean Lush, with whom I co-authored *Emotional Phases of a Woman's Life,* told about a time when she had too many things to do and not enough time. She and her family lived in a dormitory with forty-five confused and sometimes rebellious teenagers.

Jean tried to spend some quality time with each of her children, especially the youngest, Heather, who was nine. Every day they would eat breakfast together, and every night Jean would, as she says in her wonderful English accent, "dash from the big girls in the dorm to my youngest child's room. I wanted to make certain I was with her to tuck her into bed.

"One night a heard a rumor that an absolute rebellion was going to take place all over the dormitory. I was tense with worry, as I had some real characters in that bunch. Anyway, I looked at my clock and it was half-past eight, so I hurried up to my own little girl's bedroom. We had developed this little bedtime routine. Usually I'd walk in quietly, sit on the side of the bed and say something calm like, 'Well, how's your day been?' Then we would have a leisurely time with a story and prayer. We normally had about twenty minutes to half an hour."

This day, however, was anything but calm. Jean dashed into the room and said, "Heather. Are you ready for bed?

Have you brushed your teeth? Are your shoes ready for
tomorrow?" She looked around, still chattering nonstop.
"You've done your homework . . . yes. Okay, dear, jump into
bed . . . there's a good girl. Hurry up . . . Mummy's only got
a few minutes, you see . . ."

Heather stared at her mother in horror.

"Something wrong?" Jean asked, hoping to goodness
nothing was wrong. All she needed was more trouble.
When Heather didn't answer, Jean asked again, "Is something wrong here, dear?"

Heather sat on the edge of the bed and refused to get in.
Jean glanced at her watch and hurriedly said, "All right,
dear. Mother's got five more minutes. Now you tell Mum
what's the matter."

Heather didn't answer.

"Come on. Pour all your feelings out, dear. I want it fast."

With that Heather got into bed in absolute silence.

"Oh, no." Jean looked at her watch again. "Dash it all,
only three minutes." Determined to discover the source of
her daughter's distress, she breathed deeply and bent over
the bed and turned Heather over to face her. "Come now,
dear, tell Mother. Is something wrong?"

"Mummy," Heather said, "Mummy, sit down."

Obediently, Jean sat stiffly on the edge of the bed, thinking, *Oh, dear, I've got to get back to the dorm. I do wish
she'd hurry up.* Aloud she said, "Okay, dear, I'm sitting,
now tell Mother what's the matter."

"Mummy, I can't talk to you like this. Why don't you lie
down?"

Jean's five minutes were up now, so in desperation she
flattened herself on the bed, every inch stiff with mount-
ing tension.

"Mummy, I can't talk to you like that!"

"Oh dear, why not? I'm lying down like you said, right
on the bed here, so please get a move on."

"Mummy," Heather said. "Lie down in your soul."

Being too busy profoundly inhibits relationships, whether it is with God, our family members, or friends. Most of us would do well to listen to Heather's advice and *lie down in our souls.*

Growing in Faith

God accepts and loves us no matter how small our faith. I love the parable of the mustard seed (Matt. 17:20). That is all the faith we need. With that tiny seed, God can grow a tree. In the beginning faith may be difficult because we don't see God clearly. We try to catch glimpses of him through our shells and all we see are distorted images. As we grow in faith, however, our vision will clear.

Hannah Whitall Smith, in *The Unselfishness of God,* shares her account of coming to see God. After the loss of her five-year-old daughter she was consumed with sorrow. "Standing in the dark, cold prison-depths of my pain, the inner 'eyes of my soul' seemed to open slowly. I saw, as in a sudden blaze of light that, after all else is said and done, God is fact."[4]

I, too, have seen God's light. Perhaps you have as well. As you come to know God, and let the pieces of your shell fall away, you will begin to see God more clearly. Your faith will become like a rock on which you can build your life with no fear of falling.

We can come to God with little faith, but eventually, if we are to become whole and healthy, we will need a rock solid faith. The Bible tells us: "without faith it is impossible to please him, for he who comes to God must believe that he is, and that he is a rewarder of those who diligently seek him" (Heb. 11:6 NKJV).

We must believe not only that God exists, but that God can and will facilitate the changes in us that will make us whole (holy). When we grow in faith we will fully believe

Christ's words: "Take heart! I have overcome the world" (John 16:33 NIV).

As we grow in faith, we will become more and more comfortable in God's presence. "Praise be to the God and Father of our Lord Jesus Christ, the Father of compassion and the God of all comfort, who comforts us in all our troubles" (2 Cor. 1:3–4 NIV). We can be certain that discomfort means we're back to the old habit of wearing shells.

We will know that our shells are disappearing when we feel at ease with God and are able to see God's presence in our lives with increasing clarity. With the absence of our shells, we will begin to see God, not as a condemning, judgmental, and vindictive entity who's waiting for us to slip up so he can punish us, but as one who protects, nurtures, and comforts. We will make the psalmist's security our own and know too that "He will cover you with his feathers, and under his wings you will find refuge. . . . If you make the Most High your dwelling—even the LORD, who is my refuge—then no harm will befall you" (Ps. 91:4, 9–10 NIV). We will see that God gathers us to him as a mother hen gathers her chicks (Matt. 23:37). In Isaiah, the Lord says, "As a mother comforts her child, so . . . you will be comforted" (Isa. 66:13 NIV).

And we will come to see discipline as a way of love. "If love sees those it loves going wrong, it must, because it is love, do what it can to save them. Any supposed love that would fail to do this is really only selfishness."[5] Finally, we will come to see that suffering does not separate us from God, but draws us nearer.

Learning How to Suffer

Living in the Garden doesn't isolate us from problems, but it can give us courage to face them. My friend Joan is an excellent example. Joan had breast cancer about fifteen years ago, and her treatment consisted of surgical removal of one breast and radiation therapy. When she recovered, she became a volunteer in a breast cancer support group, visiting and encouraging women with similar problems. A few years later she lost her husband and oldest son in a boating accident. A short time later, doctors discovered she had a brain tumor. Then the cancer spread to her lungs and her other breast. In addition to her physical pain, she had a great deal of difficulty with her remaining children.

"One of my kids died at eighteen," Joan explained. "Another one couldn't cope with that death, blamed God, and turned to drugs. My seventeen-year-old daughter ran off with a forty-year-old married man, and they are living together. I guess you could say I know what it means to suffer. But I've never lost hope."

Joan died of the cancer but left her legacy—a philosophy about suffering that we will all do well to incorporate into our lives.

"We will all suffer, some more than others," Joan said during the final days of her illness. "When it comes, we need to walk into it, grow through it, and walk out again. It doesn't mean we pretend it isn't there, but we experience it and then get up and walk on. Like Jesus did in the Garden of Gethsemane."

I was reminded of something I'd read in William Barclay's commentary on the gospel of Luke, in which he writes about the prophetess Anna and the effect of sorrow on her life (Luke 2:36–40).

> Anna was a widow. She had known sorrow and she had not grown bitter. Sorrow can do one of two things to us. It can make us kinder, softer, more sympathetic. It can despoil us our faith; or it can root faith even deeper. It all depends on how we think of God. If we think of Him as a tyrant we will resent Him. If we think of Him as Father we too will be sure that
>> A father's hand will never cause
>> His child a needless tear.[6]

We can all make it through difficult times. One way is to know we are not alone. We can comfort one another and bear one another's burdens. Another way through is to remember God's words to us. These four Bible verses have been especially helpful for me to remember:

- "Rest in the Lord; wait patiently for him to act" (Ps. 37:7 TLB).
- "I will not leave you comfortless: I will come to you" (John 14:18 KJV).
- "Those who sow in tears shall reap in joy" (Ps. 126:5 NKJV).
- "Weeping may endure for a night, but joy comes in the morning" (Ps. 30:5 NKJV).

Being whole and healthy requires that we continually work to strengthen our relationship with God. If we are to reach our full potential, we must also care for and nurture ourselves and seek to live holy lives. But there is another important part of our development—our relationship to others.

Being God's Message

As people created in God's image, we come to understand that we are created for a purpose. We are to be more than pew warmers on Sunday mornings. As God's image bearers we are to bring God's message to a world full of hurting, broken people.

We are new creatures in Christ, filled to the brim with God's presence and overflowing with generosity and love; but are we being used? Or are we sitting behind shells nursing our wounds, working desperately to hold ourselves together? Do we hold our breath as God passes by, hoping he won't notice us, hoping that he'll call on someone else?

As we each assess our ministry—and every person has one—we need to ask ourselves some serious questions:

- What are we doing to make the church an acceptable place in which to worship?
- What are we doing to spread the gospel to our neighbors, both locally and in foreign countries?
- Do we encourage the depressed and the lonely?
- Do we heal the hurting?

Our world is full of hurting people, both inside and outside our churches. Perhaps I'm particularly sensitive to this matter because for many years I perceived the church as a sterile place filled with judgmental people who saw themselves as being above it all. I know better now, but somehow the message hasn't yet reached the masses. As God's message, we are meant to be poured-out wine and broken bread for the hurting, the hungry, and the homeless. We are to offer counsel and encouragement and to carry the load for those too weak to go on.

Our mission is not to be consistently involved in doing things, but to bring the love of Christ to the world through our very existence. Our mission is to exhibit Christ's love as we touch, hold, heal, feed, and clothe "the least of these" (Matt. 25:31–46).

What are we doing as the church—the body of Christ? Are we providing shelter and refuge for the hurting? As Morton Kelsey states, "The church is not a museum of saints but a hospital for sinners."

In *Dropping Your Guard,* Charles Swindoll says, "Churches need to be less like national shrines and more like local bars . . . less like untouchable cathedrals and more like well-used hospitals, places to bleed in rather than monuments to look at . . . places where you can have your wounds dressed."[7]

As believers and followers of Christ, we are God's message to a broken world. How are we read? Do we still reflect the image of broken humanity, or do we reflect the glory of God?

Being a whole (holy) person calls for action, not apathy. Once we offer our lives to God, he fills us with himself and we in turn are to offer whatever God has given us to help others. A wise pastor once said, "God needs us to fulfill his will on this earth. When we pray 'Thy Kingdom come, Thy will be done,' we will do well to remember that we are a way in which God brings his kingdom to earth."

People need God, and God looks to us to represent him to the world. The only Christ some people will ever see is the Christ in us.

It would take an entire book to share all of the Christlike qualities we could strive for, such as humility, discipline, and servanthood, to name a few. I can't cover them all, but before bringing this book to a close, I would like to add one more—one that makes all these qualities possible—being centered on God.

15

The Centering

I waited patiently for God to help me, then he listened and heard my cry. He lifted me out of the pit of despair, out from the bog and the mire, and set my feet on a hard, firm path and steadied me as I walked along. He has given me a new song.

Psalm 40:1–3 TLB

I WISH I COULD SAY TO YOU, "YOU'VE GOT IT MADE. Now you will live happily ever after. All you have to do is rest in the Lord." But it isn't that easy. We've come a long way in our journey toward wholeness, but we are by no means finished.

Living a holy life takes a great deal of effort. It takes effort to remain upright, to make moral and ethical choices, and to remain focused or centered on God. Being centered on God means allowing God to be the focal point in our lives. Perhaps the best way to explain is to show you how God revealed the concept of centeredness to me.

The Clay and I

One of the ways in which I survived the great fall I suffered as a result of depression was to work with my hands. My counselor suggested I take up a hobby, so I chose ceramics. There was something healing about taking a plain, gray piece of greenware and turning it into a work of art. After several years, I switched from working with greenware, which someone else had fashioned, to pottery—transforming raw clay into vases, cups, bowls, plates, honey pots, and whatever else I fancied.

I took classes, bought a wheel and kiln, and became a production potter. I loved it. Creating useable and beautiful vessels out of raw clay gave me tremendous pleasure physically, emotionally, and even spiritually.

Have you ever watched a potter working at the wheel? When I throw a pot, I take a lump of soft, shapeless clay, wedge (knead) out its air pockets and impurities, shape it into a ball, and place it in the center of the wheel.

I then moisten the clay and set the wheel in motion. The lump of clay spins with the wheel, and because it is not fully centered, it bumps and wobbles against my hand like an unbalanced top. The clay and I battle for control. As an experienced potter, I know that if the clay gives in and allows me to center it, I will be able to create out of it a symmetrical, functional vessel. I gently press the clay between my hands and ease it into the center of the wheel. Eventually, if the clay cooperates and has few flaws, I'm able to bring the clay to center.

As I encircle a centered ball of clay with my hands, I feel at one with it. It doesn't resist me, and I don't have to use force to keep it in line. The clay and its creator move as a unit, at peace with one another, with the earth, and with the universe.

When we submit in absolute surrender, we in like manner become one with our Creator God. To give you a better understanding of centeredness, let me tell you about a piece of clay that refused.

I pressed my hands against the large clay ball, struggling for control, but it resisted. Finally, in my attempts to give this clay a purpose for being, I exerted more pressure. It flew off the wheel and landed with a "splat" on the floor. I picked up the bedraggled blob, which by now had become imbedded with garage grime, and I said, "Now why couldn't you just cooperate? I had great plans for you. But no, you had to do things your way. Now it's back to the slush pile for you." I cleaned it up as best I could and tossed it into the slush bucket, which I keep by the wheel for excess clay that will eventually be reclaimed. I wondered if God had a slush bucket in which he kept his uncooperative vessels. I imagined that, like me, he also cared too much to let even one scrap of clay perish. He would, I was certain, reclaim us as many times as necessary to give each of us another chance at a purposeful life.

The potter-and-clay analogy indicates how complete our submission is to be. The analogy also points out that without God working in us, we are nothing. It is God's image in us, God's love flowing through us, and God's Spirit breathing into us that gives us validity and a reason for being. When we are centered on God, we are fortified by his strength and renewed daily by his love.

Caring for our whole selves means bursting out of and discarding our old shells. It requires that we abandon ourselves to God as children so we can experience the fullness of God's love. It means giving ourselves to God so he can guide us and design an abundant life for us.

We are like clay in that we have no say in when we are born or when we die. And certain events are out of our control, such as natural disasters and the consequences of other people's choices.

We are not like clay in that while we are living on earth, we are not passive participants in life. We are vital and alive and responsible for ourselves. We still make choices that affect our relationship with God and with others. The choices we make today can influence us and our world forever. We decide how we will live our lives.

Imagine Being One with God

It's journal time again. Find a comfortable place to relax and ask God to sit with you. Close your eyes and imagine yourself as a shapeless piece of clay being wedged and centered by the Master Potter's gentle, caring hands. Feel the cleansing water pour over you and soften you. Feel the sense of oneness when the centering is accomplished and you have submitted yourself to God. Relish the moment. Let your body relax as God forms you into a worthy vessel. Let yourself become the person God wants to form.

Write your impressions and feelings in your journal. Several years ago, when the feeling of oneness with God first came to me, I wrote this poem.

He is the potter, I, the clay.
He holds me in his hand—centers me—encircles me.
Like clay, I am weak and shapeless without the
    sustaining power of the potter's hand.
If I resist, my life becomes turmoil,
    my impurities overwhelm me.
If I submit, he nurtures me, softens me, opens me, molds
    me;
I take shape and form. I am real, full of life in
    his Holy Spirit.
Then again, if I resist I become worn and weak—I may
    break
    for my walls are thin and transparent
        as the finest porcelain.
I must submit—return to the whole, with wounds healed
    to remind me of my suffering:
        and the perfect, life-restoring God,
    who salvages me.

Being centered by God is like being converted and becoming like little children (Matt. 18:3). This is not something we do only once, but moment by moment. Once again, I'd like to share some words of wisdom from one of my favorite writers, Oswald Chambers:

> We have to be continuously converted all the days of our lives, continually turn to God as children. If we trust to our wits instead of to God, we will produce consequences for which God will hold us responsible. . . . Because we have done it once is no proof that we shall do it again. . . . There are whole tracts of our lives which have not yet been brought into subjection, and it can only be done by this continuous conversion. Slowly but surely we can claim the whole territory for the Spirit of God.[1]

Reaching Your Full Potential

Our full potential as human beings created in God's image can be achieved when we give God freedom to shape our lives. Paul said it well in Romans 12:1–2 TLB:

> And so, dear brothers [and sisters], I plead with you to give your bodies to God. Let them be a living sacrifice, holy— the kind he can accept. When you think of what he has done for you, is this too much to ask? Don't copy the behavior and customs of this world, but be a new and different person with a fresh newness in all you do and think. Then you will learn from your own experience how his ways will really satisfy you.

If we desire to live whole (holy) lives in partnership with God and be centered on him, we'll want to make choices that enhance that union. In chapter 11 I outlined God's requirements for staying whole: faithfulness, holiness, righteousness, and love. We are never forced to comply with the standards the Lord has given us. Like Adam and Eve, we decide which way we will go and how we will live.

When we come to God every day, we find ourselves more open to the direction in which God wishes to guide us. When I discovered pottery, I thought this was the answer for my life. I was to be a production potter. Finally I had a purpose, a calling. My work won awards; I had a long list of customers placing orders that I worked long, hard hours to fill. I loved it.

Then I began to feel uneasy, off balance, but I couldn't understand why. One evening as I sat at the wheel, I sensed the Lord saying, "Pat, do you love me more than these?"

I passed it off at first, thinking my imagination was working overtime. I concentrated harder on the clay in my hands. But my spirit heard the question again. "Do you love me more than these? Could you give this up for me?"

Tears welled up in my eyes and spilled onto the clay. "But God, you gave this to me," I cried. I realized in that moment that like the clay in my hands, I'd drifted off center. I had taken my focus off God and placed it on my work. In a sense, God was saying to me, "You're holding too tight. Let go."

"I'm sorry, God," I said. I closed my eyes and recentered the ball of clay in my hands, then deliberately and tearfully said yes. It hurt to have to give up my new livelihood, but I backed off from it and before long came to realize that pottery, which I still do as a hobby, was a temporary stop on my way to fulfilling God's purpose for my life—that of writing and speaking. I have been a writer since 1980, and through my writing am asked to speak at retreats, seminars, and workshops. It is a career my shell self would never have chosen, but which the new me loves. My calling thrills, satisfies, and frightens me all at the same time. For me, at least for the moment, writing and speaking are a ministry I feel certain God has called me to. God is giv-

ing me courage to speak out on important issues and pro-
claim my faith in ways I never thought possible.

We've been through a lot in this book. We've gone from
being broken to being healed and are working on becoming shell-free, integrated beings with a sense of purpose
and direction. We're learning how to live and function as
whole persons, by imitating Christ and the many followers of Christ who live holy lives and remain centered on
God. In following the Humpty analogy, we have ceased to
be broken eggs and are growing toward fullness of character, evidenced by our free spirits.

We are no longer fragile eggs but new creatures viable
and growing toward maturity. When tragedy hits, and it
will, we no longer need to feel crushed and broken. We can
rise above it. Regardless of how terrible things seem in our
world, and no matter how difficult our tasks, we can, as
Paul says, do all things through Christ who strengthens
us (Phil. 4:13).

Like the psalmist, we can sing:

> Let all who take refuge in you be glad;
> let them ever sing for joy.
> Spread your protection over them,
> that those who love your name may rejoice in you.
> For surely, O Lord, you bless the righteous;
> you surround them with your favor as with a shield.
>
> Psalm 5:11–12 NIV

Your New Life

This may be the final chapter of the Humpty Dumpty
book, but it is really only the beginning of your journey to
wholeness. The close of this book is a transition into the
next—the one you will continue to write. What will you
say? Begin with where you are now.

In closing I'd like to share a poem I wrote as a way of summing up what I have become as an integrated person who has found healing in the Lord and who is learning how to live a whole (holy) life.

When you've finished reading it, open your journal and begin writing the first chapter of your new life.

I Am

I was broken, scattered, confused
   . . . empty.
In Christ I am whole.
I am who I am—a child of God,
   woman, mother,
    artist/creator,
     lover of life—a saint.
I am body—intricately designed,
   an instrument of the mind,
    vulnerable, limited, scarred, aging
     . . . dust.
I am body—a transient miracle.
   I am body and I house the soul.
I am mind—ever seeking
   wisdom, knowledge, understanding
    . . . logic.
I am mind—cautious, disciplined, steady.
I am mind—guardian of the soul,
   seeker of truth.
I am *spirit* running free,
   wild as wind, warm as sun,
    pure as light.
I dance with my prince in the garden.
   We sit together over tea
   and laugh and cry
    together,
   Intimate as lovers in early dawn.
I am *spirit*—unfolding flower,
   scattering love's petals
    . . . at his feet.
   I lift my arms to embrace him.

He showers me with rainbows
   and eternal love.
I open to receive him
He fills my cup with living water
   and I drink.
I am *spirit,* giving birth
   to the fruits of his Spirit
   Bearing his image, I am . . .
Borne on wings of love
   warm, honest, elusive, impetuous,
   sensual.
I am *spirit* and I will live forever.

Notes

Part 1 Introduction

1. *The Annotated Mother Goose* (New York: C. N. Potter, 1962), 268.
2. Many times the condition of the spirit and the mind affect the condition of the body—physical changes can occur when the spirit and emotions are healed.

Chapter 1

1. *S.O.S. America! A Children's Defense Budget,* Children's Defense Fund, 1990, 6.
2. Lisa Levitt Ryckman, "Mom Loses Two-year-old to Stigma over Nursing," *The Oregonian,* February 4, 1992, A1–2.

Chapter 2

1. Peter Jacobi, *The Magazine Article: How to Think It, Plan It, Write it* (Cincinnati: Writer's Digest Books, 1991), 22.
2. Charles W. Carter, gen. ed., "Hamartiology: Evil, the Marrer of God's Creative Purpose and Work," *A Contemporary Wesleyan Theology,* Vol. I (Grand Rapids, Mich.: Francis Asbury Press, 1983), 208.
3. Mildred Bangs Wynkoop, *A Theology of Love* (Kansas City, Mo.: Beacon Hill Press, 1972), 107.
4. Ibid., 108.
5. William T. Kirwan, *Biblical Concepts for Christian Counseling* (Grand Rapids: Baker Book House, 1984), 81.
6. Alexander Lowen, M.D., *Narcissism: Denial of the True Self* (New York: Collier Books, Macmillan Publishing Company, 1985), ix.
7. John Bradshaw, *Bradshaw On: The Family* (Deerfield Beach, Fla.: Health Communications, Inc., 1988), 20.

Chapter 3

1. Carter, "Hamartiology: Evil, the Marrer of God's Creative Purpose and Work," 237.

2. Ibid., 239-48.

3. Ibid., 246.

4. Merrill F. Unger, *Demons in the World Today* (Wheaton, Ill.: Tyndale House Publishers, Inc., 1971), 28–29.

5. Ibid., 28.

6. For more thorough investigation of Satan and demonology, I suggest these books by Merrill F. Unger: *Demons in the World Today* (Wheaton, Ill.: Tyndale House, 1971), which includes an extensive bibliography; *What Demons Can Do to Saints,* (Chicago: Moody Press, 1978), and *Biblical Demonology* (Wheaton, Ill.: Scripture Press, 1952). Also helpful is *People of the Lie: The Hope for Healing Human Evil* by M. Scott Peck, M.D., (New York: Simon & Schuster, Inc., 1983).

7. Wayne E. Caldwell, "Angelology and Demonology: Intelligent, Non-human Creatures" in Carter, *A Contemporary Wesleyan Theology* Vol. II, 1072.

8. C. S. Lewis, *The Screwtape Letters* (New York: Macmillan, 1948), 9.

9. William T. Kirwan, *Biblical Concepts for Christian Counseling* (Grand Rapids, Mich.: Baker Book House, 1984), 86.

10. Brian W. Grant, *From Sin to Wholeness* (Philadelphia: The Westminster Press, 1982), 10.

11. Robert E. Burns, "Sin No More," U. S. Catholic, Dec. 1989, Vol. 54, No. 12, 2.

12. Grant, *From Sin to Wholeness,* 10.

13. Lou Jacquet, "Original Sin: a new look at the oldest sin in the book," *U.S. Catholic,* Vol. 54, June 1988, No. 6.

14. Grant, *From Sin to Wholeness,* 10.

Chapter 4

1. Willard B. Frick, *Personality Theories: Journeys into Self* (New York and London: Teachers College Press, 1984), 15.

2. Don Oldenburg, "Adults Confronted by Memories of Abuse," *The Washington Post,* reprinted by *The Oregonian,* 5 July 1991.

Chapter 5

1. M. Scott Peck, *The Different Drum: Community Making and Peace* (New York: Simon & Schuster, 1987), 58.

2. Gerald Corey, *Theory and Practice of Counseling and Psychotherapy, Third Edition* (Pacific Grove, CA: Brooks/Cole Publishing Company, 1986), pp. 314–15; C. B. Traux and R. R. Carkhuff, *Toward Effective Counseling and Psychotheray,* (Chicago: Aldine Publishing Company, 1967), 141.

Chapter 6

1. Carter, "Anthropology," in *A Contemporary Wesleyan Theology,* 206.

2. Madeleine L'Engle, *A Circle of Quiet* (New York: Farrar, Straus and Giroux, 1972), 63.

3. Paul DeVries, "The Deadly Sin: Unbelief is hazardous to your health, but doubt can give you hope," Christianity Today, May 15, 1987, 22.

4. Ibid., 23.

5. Ibid., 24, adapted.

6. L'Engle, 64.

Part 3 Introduction

1. Adapted from Paul Lee Tan, *Encyclopedia of 7700 Illustrations,* (Maryland: Assurance Publishers, 1988), 1216.

Chapter 7

1. L'Engle, *A Circle of Quiet,* 63.

2. David Johnson and Jeff VanVonderen, *The Subtle Power of Spiritual Abuse* (Minneapolis: Bethany House Publishers, 1991), cover matter.

3. Lith Anderson, *Dying for Change: An Arresting Look at The New Realities Confronting Churches and Para-Church Ministries* (Minneapolis: Bethany House Publishers, 1990), 111–114.

4. Wally Armbruster, *Let Me Out! I'm a Prisoner in a Stained Glass Jail* (Portland, Ore.: Multnomah Press, 1985).

5. Thomas Langford, *Practical Divinity: Theology in the Wesleyan Tradition* (Nashville: Abingdon, 1983), 41.

6. Les L. Steele, *On the Way* (Grand Rapids, Michigan: Baker Book House, 1990), 23.

Chapter 10

1. G. K. Chesterton, "What's Wrong with the World," in *The Great Thoughts* compiled by George Feldes (New York: Ballantine, 1985), 78.

2. "Feelings: Yours, Mine, and Ours," Leadership Manual, Stephen Ministers (St. Louis, Mo., 1983), 8.

3. Margery Williams, *The Velveteen Rabbit* (New York: Henry Holt, 1983), 4–5.

4. Kirwan, 80.

Chapter 11

1. Oswald Chambers, *My Utmost for His Highest* (New Jersey: Barbour and Company, Inc., 1935), 1.

Chapter 12

1. Chambers, *My Utmost for His Highest*, 36–37.

Chapter 13

1. Adapted from Charles R. Swindoll, *Growing Strong in the Seasons of Life* (Portland, Ore.: Multnomah, 1983), 312.
2. Chambers, *My Utmost for His Highest,* 10.
3. Ibid., 12.

Chapter 14

1. Chambers, *My Utmost for His Highest,* 159.
2. Harold L. Fickett Jr., *James: Faith That Works* (Glendale, Calif.: G/L Publications, 1972), 3.
3. Jacques Ellul, *Prayer and the Modern Man* (New York: Seabury Press, 1979), vi.
4. Hannah Whitall Smith, "The Unselfishness of God," as written in *Safe Within Your Love* by David Hazard (Minneapolis: Bethany House Publishers, 1992), 52.
5. Hannah Whitall Smith, "The God of All Comfort," Chap. 11, as written in *Safe Within Your Love,* 52.
6. William Barclay, *The Gospel of Luke* (Philadelphia: Westminster Press, 1975), 27.
7. Charles R. Swindoll, *Dropping Your Guard* (Waco, Tex.: Word Books, 1983), 115.

Chapter 15

1. Chambers, pp. 269–70.